Pragmatic Application of Service Management

The Five Anchor Approach

Pragmatic Application of Service Management

The Five Anchor Approach

S. D. VAN HOVE, ED.D.
MARK THOMAS, M.S.

IT Governance Publishing

Every possible effort has been made to ensure that the information contained in this book is accurate at the time of going to press, and the publisher and the author cannot accept responsibility for any errors or omissions, however caused. Any opinions expressed in this book are those of the author, not the publisher. Websites identified are for reference only, not endorsement, and any website visits are at the reader's own risk. No responsibility for loss or damage occasioned to any person acting, or refraining from action, as a result of the material in this publication can be accepted by the publisher or the author.

Apart from any fair dealing for the purposes of research or private study, or criticism or review, as permitted under the Copyright, Designs and Patents Act 1988, this publication may only be reproduced, stored or transmitted, in any form, or by any means, with the prior permission in writing of the publisher or, in the case of reprographic reproduction, in accordance with the terms of licences issued by the Copyright Licensing Agency. Enquiries concerning reproduction outside those terms should be sent to the publisher at the following address:

IT Governance Publishing
IT Governance Limited
Unit 3, Clive Court
Bartholomew's Walk
Cambridgeshire Business Park
Ely
Cambridgeshire
CB7 4EA
United Kingdom

www.itgovernance.co.uk

The authors have asserted the rights of the author under the Copyright, Designs and Patents Act, 1988, to be identified as the author of this work.

First published in the United Kingdom in 2014
by IT Governance Publishing.

ISBN 978-1-84928-514-8

FOREWORD

Will Rogers said "A man only learns in two ways, one by reading, and the other by association with smarter people." I feel like I hit "two for two" after reading this book. Written by two of the smartest people I know, Dr Suzanne Van Hove (AKA "Doc") and the debonair Mark Thomas, I knew I was onto a winner.

After almost two decades of service management experience one may be forgiven for thinking there is little left to learn about the subject; one would be wrong. There were many aha moments and much note taking as I made my way through this great handbook.

In the world of service management, practitioners and consultants alike are frequently overwhelmed with the variety of frameworks, standards and methodologies at their disposal. Gargantuan amounts of material often accompany these useful tools and wading through it takes time, a commodity most of us have in short supply these days. The authors hit their first large score here for me. Concentrating on three of the most popular approaches they have provided a succinct guide that will enable individuals and teams to get up to speed quickly.

The second big score is the focus on practicality vs. theory. Employing their unique "Five Anchor Approach" in a variety of mini case studies or "caselets", the authors demonstrate how ITIL® (a registered trademark of AXELOS Ltd), COBIT® and ISO/IEC 20000 can help companies improve. Many people will recognize challenges faced by their own organizations and will benefit from the focused solutions to common problems.

The "Doc" and Mark score again with their valuable mapping of the three techniques. As a consultant I often use all three in assessments and am frequently asked by my customers how they complement each other or whether one is a better choice over the other. The authors not only explain the ideal and purpose behind each one, but clearly show how the different parts meld together to provide a more comprehensive whole, with gaps in one being overcome by solutions in another.

If you are looking for a navigation guide to help expedite your way through the mountains of information on service management, then look no further than this book. But be warned, you will need to put a tracking device on it as it will be in high demand from your colleagues.

Jeanette Smith

Jeanette Smith
CEO, One-3-Right
Service Management Consultant
Certified to ITIL® Expert level
ISO/IEC 20000 Consultant
Accredited IT Service Management Instructor

ABOUT THE AUTHORS

Dr Suzanne D. Van Hove, Founder and CEO of SED-IT, is currently managing the consultancy and education programs of the 15-year old service management-based company. Previous life experiences focused in the educational profession – teaching at all levels, from kindergarten through post-doctoral programs. One would be hard pressed to find a professional vertical she has not touched. Dr Van Hove holds degrees from Boston University, Ithaca College and DePauw University and certifications in ITIL and ISO/IEC 20000.

Dr Van Hove managed the Knowledge Management portfolio for itSMF USA (2009-2012) and introduced the Thought Leadership series from the itSMF USA member community. She and colleague Kathy Mills produced the third book of that series, *It's All About Relationships! What ITIL Doesn't Tell You!* Dr Van Hove is an advocate for professionalism within Service Management and the inclusion of Service Management in higher education programs. In recognition of her contributions, Dr Van Hove has been awarded the itSMF USA Lifetime Achievement Award - the highest recognition of a member of itSMF USA. An opera aficionado and avid rosebush gardener, Dr Van Hove currently resides in Louisville, KY, USA.

Mark Thomas is the Founder and President of Escoute, LLC, an IT Governance consultancy as well as the previous President of the itSMF USA Kansas City LIG and COBIT SIG. As a nationally known ITIL and COBIT expert with over 20 years of professional experience, Mark's background spans leadership roles from datacenter CIO to management and IT consulting. Mark has led large teams in outsourced IT arrangements, conducted PMO, Service Management and governance activities for major project teams, and managed enterprise applications implementations across multiple industries.

Mark has a wide array of industry experience in the health care, finance, manufacturing, services, high technology, and government verticals. When he's not traveling, Mark lives with his family in the Kansas City, MO area and claims to be a 'certified' barbeque judge in his spare time.

ACKNOWLEDGEMENTS

We would like to thank the generosity of Interface Technical Training for their support of this volume. Through the use of their state-of-art recording studio, we have been able to produce a supporting video for the Five Anchor Framework. We hope you are able to view these productions within the Interface video library (*www.interfacett.com*) or through the posts on YouTube.com.

Additionally, we are grateful for the excellent work and comments from the ITG Review Committee: Brian Johnson, CA, Chris Evans, ITSM Specialist, and Dave Jones, Pink Elephant.

CONTENTS

INTRODUCTION

Thanks for picking up this book!

If you are looking for a book to help you "implement" COBIT®5, ISO/IEC 20000 or ITIL®, put this book down and go find the actual documentation from COBIT, ISO/IEC 20000 and ITIL. Frankly, this isn't the book for you.

This book addresses how to *use* COBIT5, ISO/IEC 20000-1:2011 and ITIL *together* to create a stronger and more robust Service Management System (SMS). We recognize there are many service management frameworks, standards and methodologies, including those within project management (PMI®, P30®, PRINCE2®). On purpose, we didn't include every service management framework, standard or methodology, or any of the project management frameworks for two reasons:

1. Project management deals with the planning and execution of a defined, funded and agreed plan of action.

2. We wanted to keep the book manageable:

   o Simple is effective.

This is a book on how to evaluate and assess a situation using the Five Anchor Framework and, based on that assessment, apply the guidance from COBIT5, ISO/IEC 20000-1 and ITIL to create a comprehensive improvement plan. We've provided a table at the end of the book where we have mapped COBIT5, ISO/IEC 20000-1 and ITIL to assist in the information gathering.

Use this book to *think differently*, leverage the strengths of COBIT5, ISO/IEC 20000-1 and ITIL, and mitigate the inherent weaknesses in each.

Happy Reading!

Suzanne and Mark

CHAPTER 1: WHY THIS BOOK

As independent consultants, we are constantly asked the same set of questions:

- "Aren't these frameworks for big companies only?"
- "Where do we start? What do we **have** to do?"
- "What do we measure?"
- "Is there a difference between 'prescriptive' and 'suggestive' when it comes to frameworks?"
- "Isn't ITIL (*insert any other service management framework/standard/methodology*[1]) better than COBIT (*insert any other service management framework*)?"
- "ITIL (*insert any other service management framework*) doesn't work. What else ya got?"
- "If we use multiple frameworks, how do we fit them together?"

What consistently surprises us is the prevalent "one service management body of knowledge *is better* than the others" debate. The service management community seems to have polarized to a specific framework and developed a bit of "tunnel vision." Currently, ITIL is the "most widely accepted approach to IT service management in the world."[2] As robust as ITIL is, there are areas where the information provided is either lacking or incomplete (e.g. governance, risk, implementing a working service management system, etc.). Of course, this shouldn't create a negative impression but it is an opportunity for the Service Manager to explore the other frameworks.

So, let's level set. First, all service management frameworks support the goal of delivering quality services that benefit the business efficiently, effectively and economically. This is not an unknown to anyone in the service management field. It's why

---

[1] We recognize the many service management frameworks, standards, methodologies as well as the particular nature of those terms. For ease of reading, we will use the term "framework" to represent all unless we are specifically speaking to an international standard.

[2] *www.itil-officialsite.com*

they (and their organization) have adopted and adapted the framework of their choice. However, the quandary is this: no matter what framework has been chosen, there are gaps. These gaps become more and more noticeable as one explores all available frameworks.

Second, if we agree there are gaps, we also must agree the various frameworks all have specific strengths – there is a reason why there are so many frameworks – they were developed because what was available had gaps! This is just simple logic. Service managers then need to recognize the gaps and then exploit the strengths found in the service management frameworks. As in life, there is no time or place for bigotry!

Third, most service managers have taken one or more certification classes. Well done. As good as most training is, it is not a substitute for experience. The academic deployment of framework guidance is typically doomed from the start; often creating greater disruption than the original situation which was supposed to improve with the deployment of best practice. Knowledge does not equate success.

We also recognize there will be controversy around what we have written. That is the beauty of applying frameworks – there never is an absolute. As long as one can justify, document and demonstrate the benefit sought has been achieved, there is no "wrong." Can the system improve? Absolutely and always – we are firm believers in continual improvement knowing the only constant in life is change. Thus we encourage you to look for and communicate those improvements.

The Focus

This book focuses on three of the many available frameworks – we'd love to include "all" of them but we do have to define a scope or we would never be done. Therefore, we chose (in no particular order other than alphabetical) COBIT5, ISO/IEC

20000-1:2011[3] and ITIL. We felt these three would adequately support the intent of this book and offer a solid foundation on which to build. We will offer other frameworks for consideration where appropriate and encourage you to explore them to continually improve your service management initiative. We chose these three for the following reasons:

- Availability of information
- Pervasiveness of deployment
- International acceptance
- A business need to create value
- Process orientation.

Please don't interpret the inclusion or omission of any of the many service management frameworks as a value-based decision. Each framework has a purpose and benefit. The three we've chosen creates a manageable level of information for the purpose of this book which is to show how to deploy an amalgamated solution using the strengths of each. We will use caselets (mini case studies) to provide context – each caselet is fictitious but based on real events from our consulting careers. We've chosen some rather generic and common events to demonstrate how to combine the best practices.

Strengths

While each of the frameworks is described in the next chapter, we thought it appropriate to list the strengths as we see them for these three frameworks.

- COBIT5
  - o Ability to conduct process capability assessment
  - o Metrics
  - o RACI diagrams to show interrelationships
- ISO/IEC 20000-1
  - o Concise listing of what MUST be achieved
  - o Service Management System (SMS)
- ITIL

---

[3] For ease of reading, going forward, we will refer to ISO/IEC 20000-1:2011 as ISO/IEC 20000-1.

o Well-described processes
o Generic information around lifecycle activities.

Combining these strengths, you can readily see the following benefits:

- An overall management system for the service management activities (SMS)
  o Business-based philosophy based on Deming's PCDA
- Processes to support the lifecycle service delivery
  o Interrelationships of processes for efficiency
- Descriptions of the various maturity levels within the processes (drives improvements)
  o Measuring process performance.

The Five Anchors and Caselets

Chapter 3 will hold the main content – an analysis structure, which we call the Five Anchors, developed to ensure an enterprise-wide assessment. The Five Anchors are applied to five caselets to show how to not only analyse the situations but also apply multiple frameworks towards a common goal.

When used, this analysis structure, based on practical experience as well as guidance from the service management frameworks, is a consistent view into any scenario. We've then applied various frameworks to provide information and best practices that an organization can adopt/adapt creating a solution to benefit the business.

To assist in your learning, a comprehensive mapping between COBIT5, ISO/IEC 20000-1 and ITIL, can be found in Appendix A. We recognize the 37 processes described in COBIT5 do not necessarily create a one-to-one relationship with the processes in ISO/IEC 20000-1 and ITIL. We used each framework's numbering scheme to point to specific references rather than regurgitate the information held within these frameworks. For full comprehension and to compare the information, you will need to view the full references.

CHAPTER 2: COBIT, ISO/IEC 20000 AND ITIL

While most will recognize and have in-depth knowledge of one or two of these service management philosophies, we thought it necessary to level-set not only the core structural information, but to also describe the improvement models that are integral to each framework.

Overview of COBIT5

COBIT (Control Objectives for Information and Related Technology) is a business framework for the governance and management of enterprise IT. With aspects in security, quality and compliance, its focus is not necessarily on how to execute a process, but rather what should be done to ensure proper control of that process. Therefore, you won't technically implement COBIT from the bottom up, but use it as a tool to help you control processes from the top down as a part of a larger governance initiative.

Starting out as a tool designed for IT auditors to assist in the control of IT, it has grown into a model to assist with compliance requirements as well. It helps enterprises understand IT systems, and guides decisions around the level of security, risk and control that is necessary to protect assets through the leverage of an IT governance model.

By using stakeholder needs as the starting point for governance and management activities, COBIT offers a holistic and integrated view of enterprise governance and management of IT that uses consistent and common language. This framework has many rich capabilities, notably the introduction of GEIT (Governance of Enterprise IT) principles, increased focus on enablers, new and modified processes, the separation of governance and management, revised and expanded goals and metrics, and a new process capability model to name just a few.

There are several documents and tools to choose from in the overall COBIT product family. These can be found at *www.isaca.org/cobit* and include:

- *COBIT 5, A Business Framework for the Governance and Management of Enterprise IT*[4]
- COBIT 5 Enabler Guides
  - o *COBIT 5 Enabling Processes*
  - o *COBIT 5 Enabling Information*
  - o Other Enabler Guides to be developed
- COBIT 5 Professional Guides
  - o *COBIT 5 Implementation*
  - o *COBIT 5 for Information Security*
  - o *COBIT 5 for Assurance*
  - o *COBIT 5 for Risk*
  - o Other professional guides to be developed.

The building blocks of the COBIT framework are leveraged through the use of five principles and seven enablers (see Figure 1).

- Principles
  - o Meeting Stakeholder Needs
  - o Covering the Enterprise End-to-End
  - o Applying a Single Integrated Framework
  - o Enabling a Holistic Approach
  - o Separating Governance from Management.

Note that the Principle "Enabling a Holistic Approach" gives rise to the Enablers.

- Enablers (see Figure 2)
  - o Principles, Policies and Frameworks
  - o Processes
  - o Organizational Structures
  - o Culture, Ethics and Behaviour
  - o Information
  - o Services, Infrastructure and Applications
  - o People, Skills and Competencies.

---

[4] Free to members and non-members of ISACA. All other volumes are available for purchase for non-members.

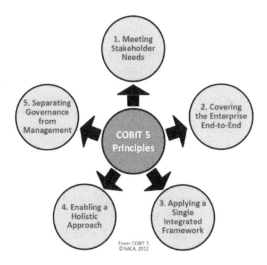

Figure 1: COBIT5 Principles

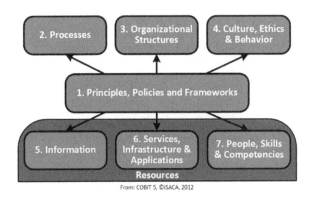

Figure 2: COBIT5 Enablers

At the core of any framework are processes. COBIT5 has 37 processes in five domains.

- **Evaluate, Direct, Monitor (EDM)** – includes processes that address stakeholder governance objectives, specifically value delivery and risk and resource optimization. Additional process activities stress the evaluation of strategic options, hence providing direction to IT. The process supporting the EDM domain include:
  o EDM 1: Ensure Governance Framework Setting and Maintenance
  o EDM 2: Ensure Benefits Delivery
  o EDM 3: Ensure Risk Optimization
  o EDM 4: Ensure Resource Optimization
  o EDM 5: Ensure Stakeholder Transparency.

- **Align, Plan & Organize (APO)** – directs solution delivery (BAI) as well as service delivery and support (DSS). Specific activities focus on strategy and tactics and how IT can impact the achievement of business objectives. These processes define the management system for IT and include:
  o APO 1: Manage the IT Framework
  o APO 2: Manage Strategy
  o APO 3: Manage Enterprise Architecture
  o APO 4: Manage Innovation
  o APO 5: Manage Portfolio
  o APO 6: Manage Budget and Costs
  o APO 7: Manage Human Resources
  o APO 8: Manage Relationships
  o APO 9: Manage Service Agreements
  o APO 10: Manage Suppliers
  o APO 11: Manage Quality
  o APO 12: Manage Risk
  o APO 13: Manage Security.

- **Build, Acquire & Implement (BAI)** – this domain provides the solutions based on the previously defined strategies and ensures the solution will support and enhance the business process. Change is also managed in this domain – again keeping the solution aligned with business objectives. The following 10 processes support the BAI objectives:

> o BAI 1: Manage Programs and Projects
> o BAI 2: Manage Requirements Definition
> o BAI 3: Manage Solutions Identification and Build
> o BAI 4: Manage Availability and Capacity
> o BAI 5: Manage Organizational change Enablement
> o BAI 6: Manage Changes
> o BAI 7: Manage Change Acceptance and Transitioning
> o BAI 8: Manage Knowledge
> o BAI 9: Manage Assets
> o BAI 10: Manage Configuration.

- **Deliver, Service & Support (DSS)** – receives the solutions and deploys the necessary functionality for the user community. The focus of DSS is on the delivery and support services including security, continuity, support services, and management of data and the environment. The processes include:
  > o DSS 1: Manage Operations
  > o DSS 2: Manage Service Requests and Incidents
  > o DSS 3: Manage Problems
  > o DSS 4: Manage Continuity
  > o DSS 5: Manage Security Services
  > o DSS 6: Manage Business Process Controls.

- **Monitor, Evaluate & Assess (MEA)** – monitors processes to ensure compliance as well as achievement of the necessary quality levels. Key areas within this domain include performance management, regulatory compliance, governance and internal control monitoring. Processes supporting these activities include:
  > o MEA 1: Monitor, Evaluate, and Assess Performance and Conformance
  > o MEA 2: Monitor, Evaluate, and Assess the System of Internal Control
  > o MEA 3: Monitor, Evaluate, and Assess Compliance with External Requirements.

These five domains support the separation of governance and management by aligning EDM with governance processes and BAI, DSS, and MEA with a typical Plan-Build-Run-Monitor approach. See Figure 3.

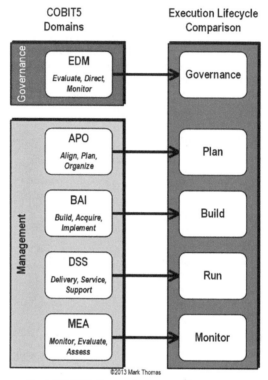

Figure 3: COBIT5 Domains to Lifecycle Activities

COBIT5

| Governance of Enterprise IT | Management of Enterprise IT | | | |
EVALUATE, DIRECT & MONITOR (EDM)	ALIGN, PLAN & ORGANIZE (APO)	BUILD, ACQUIRE & IMPLEMENT (BAI)	DELIVER, SERVICE & SUPPORT (DSS)	MONITOR, EVALUATE & ASSESS (MEA)
EDM1 Ensure Governance Framework Setting and Maintenance	APO1 Manage the IT Framework	BAI1 Manage Programs and Projects	DSS1 Manage Operations	MEA1 Monitor, Evaluate, and Assess Performance and Conformance
EDM2 Benefits Delivery	APO2 Manage Strategy	BAI2 Manage Requirements Definition	DSS2 Manage Service Requests & Incidents	MEA2 Monitor, Evaluate and Assess the System of Internal Control
EDM3 Ensure Risk Optimization	APO3 Manage Enterprise Architecture	BAI3 Manage Solutions Identification and Build	DSS3 Manage Problems	MEA3 Monitor, Evaluate and Assess Compliance with External Requirements
EDM4 Ensure Resource Optimization	APO4 Manage Innovation	BAI4 Manage Availability and Capacity	DSS4 Manage Continuity	
EDM5 Ensure Stakeholder Transparency	APO5 Manage Portfolio	BAI5 Manage Organizational Change Enablement	DSS5 Manage Security Services	
	APO6 Manage Budget & Costs	BAI6 Manage Changes	DSS6 Manage Business Process Controls	
	APO7 Manage Human Resources	BAI7 Manage Change Acceptance and Transitioning		
	APO8 Manage Relationships	BAI8 Manage Knowledge		
	APO9 Manage Service Agreements	BAI9 Manage Assets		
	APO10 Manage Suppliers	BAI10 Manage Configuration		
	APO11 Manage Quality			
	APO12 Manage Risk			
	APO13 Manage Security			

Table 1: COBIT5 Domains and Processes

ISO/IEC 20000-1:2011

The ISO/IEC 20000 family of documents define the international Standard for IT service management with a goal of establishing a common reference for IT service delivery. There are several parts to the Standard, which revolve around the auditable Part 1 (26 pages) and includes:

- Part 1: Service management system requirements
- Part 2: Guidance on the application of service management systems
- Part 3: Guidance on scope definition and applicability of ISO/IEC 20000-1
- Part 4: Process reference model [Technical Report][5]
- Part 5: Exemplar implementation plan for ISO/IEC 20000-1 [Technical Report]
- Part 6: Requirements for bodies providing audit and certification of service management systems[3]
- Part 8: Guidance on implementation of service management systems for smaller organizations[3] [Technical Report]
- Part 9: Guidance on the application of ISO/IEC 20000-1 to the cloud[6] [Technical Report]
- Part 10:Concepts and terminology [Technical Report]
- Part 11: Guidance on the relationship between ISO/IEC 20000-1:2011 and related service management frameworks [Technical Report][7].

Simply, Part 1 defines the internationally accepted requirements for the Service Management System (SMS) which include the "...design, transition, delivery and improvement of services that fulfil service requirements and provide value for both the customer and service provider."[8]

Developed originally as a UK national Standard (BS 15000), the early "edition" was a method allowing consistent measurement indicating compliance to ITIL 'best practices,'

---

[5] Under review – currently in preliminary status
[6] Under development
[7] On hold status pending ISO/ITTF decision on publication
[8] ISO/IEC 20000-1:2011, Information Technology – Service Management – Part 1: Service management system requirements

thus allowing organizations to declare themselves compliant. The international community quickly saw the benefit of BS 15000 and moved it through the process to create the international Standard, ISO/IEC 20000-1:2005. ISO/IEC 20000 continually improves following and driving ITIL improvements. Incorrectly known as the "ITIL Standard," ISO/IEC 20000 is a service management product in its own right. It demands an integrated process approach based in the PDCA methodology across all aspects of the SMS and services. Combining the SMS with the PDCA drives value-driven service delivery, customer satisfaction and monitored, reviewed and improved services based on objectives and agreed measurements.

The unique aspect of ISO/IEC 20000-1 is the definition of a service management system. A service provider must "...plan, establish, implement, operate, monitor, review, maintain and improve an SMS" throughout the span of service activities (e.g. design, transition, delivery and improvement). Specifically, the SMS includes very clear requirements for management responsibility, governance of processes operated by other parties, document and resource management, and the explicit activities of establishing and improving the SMS following the PDCA methodologies.

The SMS provides the management foundation for the well-known service management processes divided into four main groupings:

- **Service Delivery** (Service Level Management, Service Reporting, Service Continuity and Availability Management, Budgeting/Accounting, Capacity Management, Information Security Management)
- **Relationship** (Business Relationship Management, Supplier Management)
- **Resolution** (Incident and Service Request Management, Problem Management)
- **Control** (Configuration Management, Change Management, Release and Deployment Management).

Lastly, there is an overall set of requirements for the design and transition of new or changed services. This set of requirements nicely defines the flow of activities beginning with planning for the new or changed service (e.g. requirements gathering, resource management, communication, testing, dependencies, service acceptance criteria, etc.) and progressing through the design, development and transitioning of the new or changed service. Retiring an obsolete service falls under this section as well.

Part 1 is brilliant in its brevity – the requirements are concise and clear. What is not provided by Part 1 is the "how to do." Part 2 and the other Parts provide further clarification and great insight to the requirements as well as specific examples to fulfil the requirements but, again, the "how to do" is still not prescribed. It is clearly up to the organization and their unique working environment to define how to meet the requirements and then document them. ISO/IEC 20000 family of documents is, in our opinion, the place to start any information gathering for an "adopt and adapt" initiative. Then utilize the other Service Management frameworks and standards as a body of knowledge to complete the "how."

Table 2 lists the processes and the corresponding section numbering from the source document. These numbers are important to the mapping information found the Appendix.

ISO/IEC 20000-1: 2011 Processes

4 Service Management System Requirements	5 Design and transition of new or changed services	6 Service Delivery Processes	7 Relationship Processes	8 Resolution Processes
4.1 Management Responsibility	5.1 General	6.1 Service level management	7.1 Business relationship management	8.1 Incident Management
4.2 Governance of processes operated by other parties	5.2 Plan new or changed services	6.2 Service reporting	7.2 Supplier management	8.2 Problem Management
4.3 Documentation Management	5.3 Design and development of new or changed services	6.3 Service continuity and availability management		
4.4 Resource Management	5.4 Transition of new or changed services	6.4 Budgeting and accounting for services	9 Control Processes	
4.5 Establish and improve the SMS		6.5 Capacity management	9.1 Configuration Management	
4.5.1 Define Scope		6.6 Information security management	9.2 Change Management	
4.5.2 Plan the SMS (Plan)			9.3 Release and deployment management	
4.5.3 Implement and operate the SMS (Do)				
4.5.4 Monitor and review the SMS (Check)				
5.4.4 Maintain and improve the SMS (Act)				

Table 2: ISO/IEC 20000 Processes

Overview of ITIL

The Information Technology Infrastructure Library (ITIL) describes a framework of best practices for the provision of quality services. ITIL is only one of part of a suite of publications that describe IT service management. The activities, processes, functions and capabilities documented in ITIL provide guidance that should be analysed by an organization to define an 'adopt and adapt' program of activities to improve service delivery based on their individual needs, culture, organizational structure, and so on. The use of public frameworks and standards benefit the organization as the "wheel isn't reinvented" and the organization can create their own efficiencies from what has already been learned.

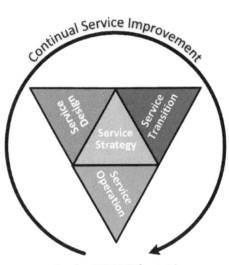

Based on AXELOS ITIL® material

Figure 4: The ITIL Lifecycle

ITIL® Service Lifecycle Publications, 2011 Edition

So where do these 'best practices' originate? ITIL is based on various sources (e.g. standards, industry practices, academic research, training and education and internal experience) though the work of a variety practitioners (e.g. employees, customers, suppliers, advisers and technologies). Business requirements (e.g. legal, regulatory, customers, corporate mission, etc.) create knowledge that is fit for business purposes and has defined objectives, a specific context and measurable purpose.

As a 'public domain' set of best practices, the information held within ITIL is more likely to be used and improved via use and as such, offers an advantage over proprietary knowledge and processes. Thus, a great deal of the success of ITIL has been due to the fact that the information has been readily and easily available and the vocabulary used in the books has found general acceptance. Additionally, ITIL is vendor-neutral, non-prescriptive and represents best practices from industry leaders of best-in-class service providers. Adopting ITIL enables organizations to:

- Deliver value to customers through services
- Integrate service strategy with business strategy and customer need
- Measure, monitor and optimize IT services
- Manage risk
- Manage knowledge
- Manage capabilities and resources
- Adopt a standard approach to Service Management
- Change organizational culture to support achievement of sustained success
- Improve interaction and relationships with customers
- Optimize and reduce cost.

ITIL is based on the concept of a five-stage service lifecycle. A brief description of each stage is below:

- **Service Strategy (SS)** – strategy is the source of value creation as it is grounded in the understanding of organizational objectives and customer needs. Concepts such as provider types, market spaces, service assets, and the service portfolio are critical to this lifecycle stage. Processes supporting SS include:
  - o Strategy Management for IT Services (StM)
  - o Service Portfolio Management (SPM)
  - o Financial Management for IT Services (FM)

o Demand Management (DM)
o Business Relationship Management (BRM)

- **Service Design (SD)** – the stage that turns the service strategy into plans that will deliver business objectives. Key concepts of design and development, management systems, technology and architecture, process design and designing measurement systems are central to the activities within SD. Processes supporting these activities include:
  o Design Coordination (DC)
  o Service Catalogue Management (SCatM)
  o Service Level Management (SLM)
  o Availability Management (AM)
  o Capacity Management (CapM)
  o IT Service Continuity Management (ITSCM)
  o Information Security Management (ISM)
  o Supplier Management (SuppM)

- **Service Transition (ST)** – focuses on the processes necessary to deliver new or changed services (or removing a service) with the fundamental purpose of controlling risk. ST ensures the value identified in SS is effectively transitioned to operation. Processes that support the ST activities include:
  o Transition Planning and Support (TPS)
  o Change Management (ChM)
  o Service Asset and Configuration Management (SACM)
  o Release and Deployment Management (RDM)
  o Service Validation and Testing (SVT)
  o Change Evaluation (ChE)
  o Knowledge Management (KM)

- **Service Operation (SO)** – includes the "visible" activities of the service provider – the agreed, designed and transitioned services are now available (visible). The activities and processes of SO all focus on the concept of value delivery not only to the customer and user, but also the service provider. Both proactive and reactive activities dominate this stage, again with the purpose of meeting the current and future needs of the business and service provider alike. Processes and functions (in italics) that support the SO activities include:
  o Event Management (EM)

o Incident Management (IM)
o Request Fulfilment (RF)
o Problem Management (PM)
o Access Management (AccM)
o *Service Desk*
o *Technical Management (TM)*
o *IT Operations Management (ITOpsM)*
o *Application Management (AppM)*

- **Continual Service Improvement (CSI)** – focuses on the activities that support improvement initiatives within strategy, design, transition and operational activities. Using principles and practices from quality management, CSI links improvement activities to the ongoing needs of the business. Grounded in Deming's Plan-Do-Check-Act (PDCA) methodology, CSI concentrates on elements of service measurement, reporting and assessments.
  o 7-Step Improvement Process (7S)

More information around ITIL and its educational schema can be found at *www.itil-officialsite.com*.

Table 3 lists the processes and the corresponding section numbering from the source documents. These numbers are important to the mapping information found the Appendix.

ITIL

Processes and Functions

SS Service Strategy	**SD** Service Design	**ST** Service Transition	**SO** Service Operation	**CSI** Continual Service Improvement
4.1 Strategy Management for IT Services (StM)	**4.1** Design Coordination (DC)	**4.1** Transition Planning & Support (TPS)	**4.1** Event Management (EM)	**4.1** Seven Step Improvement (7S)
4.2 Service Portfolio Management (SPM)	**4.2** Service Catalog Management (SCatM)	**4.2** Change Management (ChM)	**4.2** Incident Management (IM)	
4.3 Financial Management for IT Services (FM)	**4.3** Service Level Management (SLM)	**4.3** Service Asset and Configuration Management (SACM)	**4.3** Request Fulfillment (RF)	
4.4 Demand Management (DM)	**4.4** Availability Management (AM)	**4.4** Release and Deployment Management (RDM)	**4.4** Problem Management (PM)	
4.5 Business Relationship Management (BRM)	**4.5** Capacity Management (CapM)	**4.5** Service Validation & Testing (SVT)	**4.5** Access Management (AccM)	
	4.6 IT Service Continuity Management (ITSCM)	**4.6** Change Evaluation (ChE)	Functions	
	4.7 Information Security Management (ISM)	**4.7** Knowledge Management (KM)	**6.3** Service Desk	
	4.8 Supplier Management (SuppM)		**6.4** Technical Management	
			6.5 IT Operations Management	
			6.6 Application Management	

Table 3: ITIL Lifecycle Processes and Functions

Improvement Models

IT Governance Implementation Model

Within *COBIT 5 Implementation*, the "Implementation Life Cycle" is the core concept and is key to the COBIT5 framework. This reference guide provides a good practice approach to continual improvement that can be used to implement the various components of a governance framework. As with all improvement lifecycles, it can be tailored to meet specific enterprise needs.

It is well-known that any improvement initiative should be driven by the business need of creating value, and to ensure that this value is realized, adoption of efforts should be viewed from several different perspectives. Additionally, efforts should have the right mix of sponsorship, proper scope, well-understood objectives, and should fit the overall appetite for change that the enterprise can absorb.

The implementation lifecycle, illustrated in Figure 5, provides a methodology for organizations to leverage clearly defined (iterative) steps to adopt the COBIT framework. The three interrelated components and their associated steps are shown in the following table.

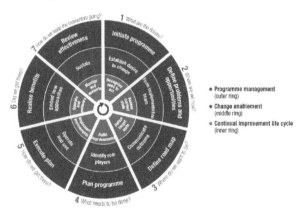

- Programme management (outer ring)
- Change enablement (middle ring)
- Continual improvement life cycle (inner ring)

Figure 5: The Implementation Lifecycle
***COBIT5 Implementation Guide*, ISACA**

COBIT5 Implementation Model

Interrelated Components and their Associated Steps

	Phase 1 — What are the drivers?	Phase 2 — Where are we now?	Phase 3 — Where do we want to be?	Phase 4 — What needs to be done?	Phase 5 — How do we get there?	Phase 6 — Did we get there?	Phase 7 — How do we keep the momentum going?
Program Management (PM)	Initiate program	Define problems and opportunities	Define roadmap	Plan program	Execute plan	Realize benefits	Review effectiveness
Change Enablement (CE)	Establish desire to change	Form implementation team	Communicate outcome	Identify role players	Operate and use	Embed new approaches	Sustain
Continual Improvement Lifecycle (CI)	Recognize need to act	Assess current state	Define target state	Build improvements	Implement improvements	Operate and measure	Monitor and evaluate

Table 4: Table 4: Interrelated Components and their Associated Steps

This approach clearly indicates that all three components need to be addressed and that they are interrelated – any major improvement effort (like the deployment of a new or changed service or process) requires the control that good program management will bring as well as some changes within the organization, specifically, understand and addressing the organizational change tolerance as well as developing and enhancing the cultural environment for continual improvement. There are seven phases; each defining a main activity within that component. The seven phases are:

- **Phase 1: What are the drivers?** Identifies the need for improvement by capturing and addressing change drivers and trigger events (pain points) and subsequently, creates a desire to change from an executive level, documented in a business case.
- **Phase 2: Where are we now?** The focus of this phase is defining current capability by defining enterprise and IT-related goals via the Goals Cascade. These elements will guide a process capability assessment, with the end result answering "where we are now" based on the pre-defined desired state.
- **Phase 3: Where do we want to be?** Improvement targets are set based on the process capability assessment. These results will define the gap between the as-is and the to-be state which identify improvement opportunities.
- **Phase 4: What needs to be done?** Improvement solutions are documented noting that some may be very quick wins and others may have much longer implementation timelines. Define the projects based on priority of the projects overall contribution to overall business objectives.
- **Phase 5: How do we get there?** Deploy the practical solution meeting the various objectives defined in the previous steps. Ensure good measures are defined, deployed and monitored to ensure continued alignment with business objectives as well as continued engagement of top management and other stakeholders.
- **Phase 6: Did we get there?** Continue monitoring and ensure no recidivism in order to achieve the expected benefits.

- **Phase 7: How do we keep the momentum going?**
Review the program success, any new governance or management requirements and reinforce the need for continual improvement.

PDCA

Many process-based management systems (i.e. ISO9001, ISO/IEC 20000, ISO/IEC 27001, etc.) are underpinned by the Deming Cycle (Plan-Do-Check-Act - PDCA). The power of this methodology is in its absolute simplicity – four easy to understand steps that drive continual review and assessment of a process or activity. Briefly, PDCA can be condensed as such:

- **Plan** – objectives, policies, plans are defined for a process, service, system.
- **Do** – implement the process, service, system.
- **Check** – monitor and measure the activities and outcomes against the objectives, policies and requirements; report on the results.
- **Act** – based on the assessed results, take actions to improve the performance.

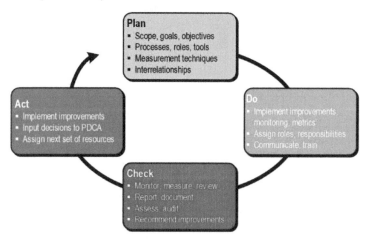

Figure 6: Deming's PDCA

PDCA is meant to be iterative with each cycle moving the process closer and closer to the defined "ultimate" goal. What is interesting is that the success of PDCA is based on the capture of knowledge from previous iterations. This increase of knowledge within each iteration allows one to refine the ultimate goal, which may very well be an initial "best guess," to something that is more appropriate and focused on true business need. This methodology allows for movement where the sometimes overwhelming "ready, aim, aim, aim, aim, aim...." actions of getting it "perfect" the first time and never accomplishing anything are now replaced with a "ready, aim, fire, aim, fire" action. Between each "aim, fire" sequence, the lessons learned are applied to the next. This is more "forgiving" than having a specific, "set in stone" goal that on paper, is fantastic but when operationalized, very unrealistic. Now, learning and improvement are a constant rather than a side-effect of, possibly, a very expensive and limited value exercise.

PDCA underpins the activities and processes of the Service Management System (SMS) as described in ISO/IEC 20000-1. Also, it is quite easy to see where the ITIL Service Lifecycle holds the PDCA elements:

- **Plan** – Service Strategy and Service Design
- **Do** – Service Transition
- **Check** – Service Operation
- **Act** – Continual Service Improvement.

CSI Approach

One improvement method found within the 2011 ITIL literature is the CSI Approach (formally CSI Model or CSI Plan). This approach can be summarized in six steps (see figure 7):

- **What is the vision?** – understand the high-level business objectives, the organizational culture and environment (is it ready to or can it embrace the changes?), ensure the alignment of business and IT strategies, specifically linking the improvement to the benefit and support of the organizational directions.
- **Where are you now?** – complete a baseline maturity assessment against a known standard or benchmark

(ISO/IEC 20000-1, COBIT, SWOT analysis, etc.) where people (skills and competencies; values and beliefs), process, products (technology and tools) and partners (suppliers and partners) are fully analysed.

- **Where do you want to be?** – agree and prioritize the improvements that represent the steps necessary to achieve the vision thus setting specific goals and objectives (SMART) across the enterprise within a manageable timeframe.
- **How do we get there?** – implement a detailed plan based on the improvements previously defined to improve service and process quality.
- **Did we get there?** – define a series of measurements and metrics to measure progress to the agreed milestones, but also ensure compliance to the new process or service activities.
- **How do we keep the momentum going?** – using measures and metrics, organizational change techniques and good management to ensure changes become embedded in the organization and there is no opportunity or tolerance for recidivism and then start the cycle again – review vision and objectives, identify new improvements, etc.

Deming's PDCA can easily be seen in this model with the first three steps fulfilling "Plan" and then the remaining steps match up directly with the final three Deming components.

This approach is valid in any and every aspect of the business. Frankly, we have followed this model on our consulting engagements – it's clear and simple and it demands a focus on the business need, thus providing value for the customer and service provider. Apply this model not only to in-place services and functions but also to the ones that are only in the planning or 'pre-planning' stages. Following this specific model can prevent design flaws, provide focus for strategic activities, and improve transition measures and on-going operational activities because the focus is on the end goal – achievement of business outcome. The question "how does the proposed improvement allow for the achievement of organizational goals?" is now definitively answered.

Based on AXELOS ITIL® material

Figure 7: CSI Approach

ITIL® Service Lifecycle Publications, 2011 Edition

Summary

We think it is fairly clear that these three improvement models have a bit of overlap. The main point here is that as a service manager you adopt and adapt a model – be it the Implementation Lifecycle, Deming or the CSI Approach, or one of the many other models available. Or better yet, create something that works for you and your clients, always remembering the many elements to consider to ensure a robust improvement.

CHAPTER 3: THE FIVE ANCHORS

Before we dive into the caselets, there is a core set of information applied to each caselet which guides a potential "solution." We call this framework the **Five Anchors** and it revolves around a series of 15 questions in five key areas. These questions (numbered below) allow you to focus on fundamental management areas from an enterprise perspective. Each question is further expanded in the bullets. The breadth of these questions allow the user to look "full scope" rather than risking a constrained focus (e.g. the stereotypic knee-jerk reaction towards technology solutions).

The Five Anchors

I. **Strategic Alignment: IT Services to Business Objectives**
   1. What are the business strategy, goals and objectives?
      What are the measures that demonstrate the achievement of the business strategy, goals and objectives?
      o This information should be gathered *before* any improvement initiative begins so the solution to the issue is based on business need. *Additionally, measures (CSFs, KPIs) should be defined, understood and deployed at this point in order to create the necessary baseline to show improvements.*
   2. What is the business issue or activity at risk?
      o Is a vital business function at risk, is it a new market activity, or is there a high degree of urgency and/or impact (priority)?
   3. Is the ownership to resolve the situation (caselet scenario) at the appropriate level of authority?
      o The solution set or current situation should be addressed by an accountable named role, therefore, is that role the decision-authority?

II. Security, Compliance, and Risk Issues

1. Has there been a compromise of the information security policy?
   o Review the confidentiality, integrity and accessibility of information resources and ensure the business issue has not breached the approved and/or agreed information security policy (protect business interest).
2. What are the internal and external compliance or regulatory concerns?
   o Apply an appropriate balance among the relevant regulatory, statutory and contractual obligations to ensure business outcomes are met (performance and conformance).
3. What is the cultural appetite for risk?
   o Define and agree with key stakeholders the organizational risk tolerance, understanding that risk tolerance may differ among departments, services, entities, etc.

III. Value-based Portfolio

1. Does the current portfolio meet expectations and needs of the stakeholder?
   o Does the service provider have the necessary resources and capabilities to create the necessary level of customer satisfaction (business outcomes, preferences and perceptions)?
2. What is the value of that business activity (VBF)?
   o Use the outcome of a Business Impact Analysis (BIA), SWOT analysis (Strengths, Weaknesses, Opportunities, Threats), PESTEL analysis (Political, Economic, Social, Technological, Environmental, Legal), etc., to understand the impact of the situation and classify appropriately. If we understand the value and impact of the activity in terms of the business need, we can deploy the correct resources and capability.
3. Does the portfolio have the right mix of resources to deliver business benefit?
   o Link portfolio resources to the defined IT and business strategies to ensure ROI/VOI. This entails balancing the appropriate investment mix which links current strategies to financial resources.

IV. **Design and Architecture**
1. Will the current architecture effectively resolve the situation? Is it feasible?
   o Define the current architectural layers (i.e. business process, information, data, application, technology) and are those layers feasible to support the current situation?
2. Can the current architecture accommodate the situation?
   o Is the current architecture flexible, scalable, available, reliable, resilient, usable, maintainable, secure, affordable, etc.?
3. Do we have the necessary competencies to design the required change(s)?
   o Do current staff, internal or consultants, have the necessary skills, knowledge, information and experience or expertise to meet the design requirements?

V. **Planning and Use of Resources**
1. What resources are required to resolve the situation (e.g. people, capital, technical…)?
   o Begin the planning process and list all potential resources to resolve the situation – think from an idyllic perspective and then let organizational constraints filter that list to an acceptable solution set.
2. Can the required resources be acquired?
   o Evaluate current resource capability toward meeting desired objectives versus a procured external solution ("build vs. buy").
3. Is the necessary data and information available, collected and managed to resolve the current situation and prevent future occurrence?
   o Is information managed from creation to retirement?

Structure

In the following chapters, we present five unique caselets that represent common issues in the following general areas:

- Governance
- Resource optimization

- Risk Management
- Achievement of business outcomes
- Compliance and/or Improvement

In each of the caselets, we have applied the Five Anchors and documented our thoughts based on the caselet around each anchor. If appropriate, we have listed sections from COBIT5, ISO/IEC 20000 and ITIL that would support or clarify the situation. We have used section numbers only for clarity – major section numbers have been provided in tables in the preceding chapters. Lastly, based on the analysis, we have applied one of the improvement models and defined the key steps required for successful resolution.

CHAPTER 4:
CASELET #1 - GOVERNANCE

IT Issue: An international import/export company is expecting significant growth over the next two years. The Board of Directors recently held a two-day retreat, during which they created an IT Governance Committee. This was in response to the growing reliance on IT systems, their interoperability, and the overall past performance of the IT organization. The IT Governance Committee met for the first time last month and convened with the following areas that needed further study:

- What vital business processes are dependent on IT and what are their requirements?
- How much of the IT effort is spent on fighting fires rather than enabling the business?
- Do we have sufficient IT resources and infrastructure to meet the strategic objectives of the business?
- Have we addressed all non-minor IT-related risks?

The VP of IT has been asked to create a presentation for the next IT Governance Committee meeting to address the above concerns and suggest action plans to address any shortcomings or gaps.

The Five Anchors

Anchor	Discussion
I. Strategic Alignment: IT Services to Business Objectives	
1. What are the business strategy, goals and objectives? *Are there any measures that demonstrate the achievement of the business strategy, goals and objectives?*	• No matter what the business issue or scenario you're trying to improve, you *must* always know the business strategy, goals and objectives. If you do not have a process in place that drives IT activity through business strategy, goals and objectives,

Anchor	Discussion
	review: • **COBIT5**: Goals Cascade • **ISO20K**: Implied through the fulfillment of service requirements (4.0) • **ITIL**: SS 4.1, 5.1.1; SD 3.1.6, 3.5; CSI 3.10
2. What is the business issue, or activity at risk?	• In order to meet the projected growth, IT systems must change their philosophy and design parameters to meet the new business requirements not only for the growth but also resilience and security concerns. • **COBIT5**: Goals Cascade, EDM03 • **ISO20K**: 4.0, 6.3, 6.5, 6.6 • **ITIL**: SD 4.4, 4.5, 4.7
3. Is the ownership to resolve the issue at the appropriate level of authority?	• While the VP of IT has been tasked with the reporting, we can assume also tasked with the responsibility and/or accountability that the necessary changes are made. We do not have enough information to confirm this action. • What we do know is that the Board created a Governance Committee who has delegated the responsibility of resolving the situation to the IT leadership which is consistent with the COBIT5 enabler "Organizational Structures."

Anchor	Discussion
II. Security, Compliance, and Risk Issues	
1. Has there been a compromise of the information security policy?	• N/A
2. What are the internal and external compliance or regulatory concerns?	• As an international import/export company, we can assume there are regulatory, legal, and perhaps contractual obligations. As a general rule, we would ensure these constraints would be considered and mitigated in any improvement design. • **COBIT5**: APO11, MEA03
3. What is the cultural appetite for risk?	• Because there is active executive involvement by the Board, there is an understanding that IT risks be documented and addressed. A specific request for plans around addressing all IT-related risks is an outcome, therefore, even though it is not stated in the caselet, the assumption is low risk tolerance. • **COBIT5**: EDM03, APO12 • **ITIL**: SS 5.6.5, D.3, E
III. Value-based Portfolio	
1. Does the current portfolio meet expectations and needs of the stakeholder?	• Assumed, yes; but will the current portfolio meet the needs of the future business direction? • **COBIT5**: APO05 • **ISO20K**: 5.0 • **ITIL**: SS 4.2
2. What is the value of that business activity (VBF)?	• While there is not a specific service described, the overall activities of IT must meet the future growth, security, and

Anchor	Discussion
	availability needs.
	• Review "Strategic Alignment", question #2 above
3. Does the portfolio have the right mix of resources to deliver business benefit?	• The assumption is "yes" because outsourcing has not been mentioned by the Governance Committee. That doesn't mean in the report by the VP of IT, in answering the Committee's concerns, that outsourcing is not an option for consideration in meeting future requirements.
	• **COBIT5**: EDM02, EDM04, APO05
	• **ITIL**: SS 3.7; SD 3.11
IV. Design and Architecture	
1. Will the current architecture effectively resolve the issue? Is it feasible?	• This issue must be addressed to meet the utility and warranty needs of the organization. The current architecture appears to effectively meet the needs now, but given the planned growth, a detailed assessment is required to ensure support of future business strategy. Data and information gathered from Technical and Application Management teams provide the necessary input.
	• **COBIT5**: APO03
	• **ITIL**: SO 6.4, 6.6
2. Can the current architecture accommodate the issue?	• At this point, no information to the contrary is available.
3. Do we have the necessary	• VP of IT is responsible for the response to the Governance

Anchor	Discussion
competencies to design the required change(s)?	Committee. There is no definite indication in the caselet that the necessary competencies are not available.
V. Planning and Use of Resources	
1. What resources are required to resolve the situation (e.g. people, capital, technical...)?	• Unknown with the information provided.
2. Can the required resources be acquired?	• N/A but assuming the support is available if only through the enterprise-based questions from the Governance Committee and recognition of increased reliance on IT systems.
3. Is the necessary data and information available, collected and managed to resolve the current situation and prevent future occurrence?	• Unknown with the information provided.

Improvement Model Application

This scenario can be resolved by following any of the three improvement models but we will focus on just two: ITIL's CSI Model and COBIT's Implementation Model. This caselet demands a review of what is currently in place and then an examination of the gap between now and what is needed. If we focus on the first three steps of the CSI Model and COBIT's Implementation Model, we effectively ensure we address the organization strategies, goals and objectives and capture an unbiased view of "now" and clearly delineate the gap to the "future."

Solution References:

Primary Solution:

COBIT5: The main source of information will come from the Goals Cascade and two domains: EDM and APO. But, to get to those domains and processes, we strongly encourage you to utilize the Goals Cascade, which can be found in *COBIT 5: A Business Framework for the Governance and Management of Enterprise IT* (pg. 18). The Goals Cascade directly relates to Principle 1 "Meeting Stakeholder Needs" which is a foremost concern in this caselet. The *Business Framework* document is not member-only information and can be freely downloaded at *www.isaca.org*.

To summarize how the goals cascade flows, the general steps to conduct in this exercise include:

- Understanding the stakeholder drivers, and map them to stakeholder needs
- Cascade stakeholder needs to Enterprise Goals
- Cascade Enterprise Goals to IT-Related Goals
- Cascade IT-related Goals to Enabler Goals
- Determine appropriate processes (particularly from the EDM and APO domains).

Secondary Solution

ISO/IEC 20000 and ITIL are underpinned by the need for overall governance and risk management, but neither has defined risk management processes or governance mandates. Both frameworks address these elements at different levels and from different perspectives, therefore directing us to use COBIT5 as the primary solution. Elements from these models should be reviewed and incorporated as needed to resolve the situation based on the culture and environment to the organization. We have listed areas within the Five Anchors discussion that point you to specific references. We will not repeat them here.

CHAPTER 5:
CASELET #2 - RESOURCE OPTIMIZATION

IT Issue: A managed service provider delivers outsourced IT services for mid-market companies primarily in the manufacturing sector. This is a multi-tenant provider with two primary data centres. Reacting to a market opportunity identified by the Board nine months ago, this company hastily launched a new major SaaS offering in order to gain market share.

The company conducted a vendor selection for the core functionality and contracted with multiple consultants to complete the customization required to provide the value-add aspects of the new service. Many key resources were reassigned to the new effort with little backfilling. In an effort to save costs, many infrastructure decisions were deferred, opting to simply use as much of the current infrastructure capacity as possible to support the rollout. There was very little demand planning used to understand usage patterns or growth estimates.

Since the launch of the new service, multiple issues have surfaced:

- Customers have complained that the performance of the service is slow and the user experience is poor.
- Tier one support staff are overwhelmed with issues and requests that cannot be resolved at their level and must be escalated to the vendor, resulting in missed service levels.
- Other key areas of the IT function are understaffed due to the reassignment of key talent to support the SaaS launch, causing customer complaints in areas that were previously efficient.

The Five Anchors

Anchor	Discussion
I. Strategic Alignment: IT Services to Business Objectives	
1. What are the business strategy, goals and objectives? *Are there any measures that demonstrate the achievement of the business strategy, goals and objectives?*	• From a high-level, this organization is trying to gain market share as quickly as possible by launching SaaS services. This is a classic example of "Shoot, Shoot, Shoot, Ready, Aim." There really is no definite strategy for these actions. Obviously some sort of a management system is needed as well as a concerted effort to define and control actions. • **COBIT5**: APO02 • **ISO20K**: Implied through the fulfillment of service requirements (4.0) • **ITIL**: SS 3.4, 4.1; SD 3.5
2. What is the business issue, or activity at risk?	• The very real threat is to the ongoing service delivery and customer satisfaction. Worst scenario, this managed service provider is at risk for continued solvency.
3. Is the ownership to resolve the issue at the appropriate level of authority?	• Unknown with the information provided.
II. Security, Compliance, and Risk Issues	
1. Has there been a compromise of the information security	• The threat is very real, but it is unknown. We may be able to assume that since there have

Anchor	Discussion
policy?	been no security incidents, that this is not a major factor. More data and information would be necessary to definitively answer this question.
2. What are the internal and external compliance or regulatory concerns?	• This is a multi-tenant service provider with multiple contracts. We do not know the type of service or level of regulatory controls (i.e. PCI/DSS, HIPPA, SOX, SSAE, etc.) but we would certainly address those legal and/or statutory requirements or other contractual obligations to provide a scope of operations for the improvement efforts.
3. What is the cultural appetite for risk?	• Obviously it's recklessly high and perhaps management needs to step back a bit and redefine their service delivery and management to better fit the SaaS environment.
III. Value-based Portfolio	
1. Does the current portfolio meet expectations and needs of the stakeholder?	• At this point, the answer is "No" and it is based on customer feedback and staffing issues. This is an area that needs defined improvements. • **COBIT5**: EDM02, APO05 • **ISO20K**: 4.4, 7.1 • **ITIL**: SS 3.5, 4.2, 4.5; SD 3.4, 3.5
2. What is the value of that business activity (VBF)?	• It is their line of business, thus this SaaS service requires absolute control and management.

Anchor	Discussion
3. Does the portfolio have the right mix of resources to deliver business benefit?	• At this point in time, perhaps, but they are not being managed or optimized for customer or service provider benefit. Management needs to define the necessary level of competencies to support the SaaS service as well the other services in their catalog. Appropriate relationship management with the customer needs to be improved (e.g. relationship managers, better training, better information on the new service, etc.). • **COBIT5**: EDM04, APO07, APO08 • **ISO20K**: 4.1, 4.4, 7.1 • **ITIL**: SS 4.5, SD 4.5, 6.5, C.12
IV. Design and Architecture	
1. Will the current architecture effectively resolve the issue? Is it feasible?	• No. The current architecture did not consider any forecasted demand which is causing the current issues. Therefore, logically, new plans to support the SaaS service as well as improve the delivery of all services to restore customer confidence and satisfaction must be developed and deployed. • **COBIT5**: APO03, APO09, APO10, BAI04 • **ISO20K**: 6.1, 6.3, 6.5, 7.2 • **ITIL**: SD 3.4, 3.5, 4.1, 4.3, 4.4, 4.5, 4.8; ST 4.2
2. Can the current architecture accommodate the issue?	• No, see directly above.

Anchor	Discussion
3. Do we have the necessary competencies to design the required change(s)?	• Unknown – staff were moved to address the new initiative and external consultants were also used. Knowledge transfer did not occur nor were staff backfilled when they were moved. A serious look must be made around the necessary resources to continue to deliver all services. • **COBIT5**: APO07 • **ISO20K**: 4.4, 4.5.2, 4.5.3, 5.2, 5.3 • **ITIL**: SD 4.5, 6.5, N.12 • **SFIA** (*www.sfia.org.uk*): SFIA is an internationally accepted framework around skills and competencies within IT, matching areas of work to levels of responsibility. It is a wonderful tool for organizational skills management.
V. Planning and Use of Resources	
1. What resources are required to resolve the situation (e.g. people, capital, technical...)?	• A full review of all resources (e.g. people, capital, technical, etc.) is required. • **COBIT5**: APO07 • **ISO20K**: 4.4 • **ITIL**: SD 4.5; ST 4.2
2. Can the required resources be acquired?	• Of course. To ensure efficiency and economics, competencies and an accurate technical design are required *BEFORE* resources are procured. • **COBIT5**: APO07 • **ISO20K**: 4.4, 4.5.2, 4.5.3, 5.2, 5.3 • **ITIL**: SD 4.5

Anchor	Discussion
3. Is the necessary data and information available, collected and managed to resolve the current situation and prevent future occurrence?	• We certainly know what's wrong, but now we need to act in an efficient, effective and economic manner. The "shoot from the hip" actions that created the SaaS service must be curtailed and a process to support all services and service provider activities must be created. • **COBIT5**: BAI08, Information Enabler • **ITIL**: ST 4.7; CSI 3.9

Improvement Model Application

Deming's PDCA comes to mind immediately in this situation – planning was omitted and now there are definite issues. To correct, the plans to support the SaaS service, as well as the remaining service catalogue, must be created to ensure not only the technology is addressed – address staff competencies as well as their roles and responsibility. Deploy (do) this plan in an organized and controlled fashion to mitigate impact on current service delivery (as bad as it is – don't make it worse!). Lastly, as plans are developed, ensure there are quality measures (check) in place to enable clear reporting on the performance of the services from a technology and a customer satisfaction view. Act on those reports and deploy improvements as needed.

ISO/IEC 20000-1:2011 and ISO/IEC 20000-2:2012 offer clear and concise guidance around PDCA. Additionally, this information is coupled with the overall concept of a service management system, further reinforcing the need to clearly define leadership roles, policies and communication. *Design and transition of new and changed services* (Clause 5) offers a high-level overview of moving from a concept to an operational service in production. These activities are clearly under the control of Change Management highlighting the need for a strong Change Management process – not Change Scheduling! Clauses 5.2-5.4 provide the areas for consideration not only for the development of the plan and supporting policies for the

SaaS service, but also the activities for design, development and transition.

Solution References:

Primary Solution:

ISO20K: *Establish and Improve the SMS* (4.5) definitively details the PDCA actions required for ongoing management and improvement of the SMS. Consider each area, analyse its efficacy within the organization, and define an improvement program.

Secondary Solution:

ITIL: Within the pages of ITIL Service Design, the Five Aspects of Service Design (service solution, management information systems, technology architectures and tools, processes and measures and metrics) provide a technological view of a new or changed service. These aspects are supported by the processes listed above with a direct concentration on overall management (DC) as well as the remaining design-oriented processes (AM, CapM, ITSCM, ISM, SuppM).

COBIT5: Confirm the objectives via the Goals Cascade and review the information around APO07 and BAI08. Incorporate the relevant pieces into the improvement plans.

CHAPTER 6:
CASELET #3 - RISK MANAGEMENT

IT Issue: A candy manufacturer conducted a selection process for a major ERP replacement system. The implementation was supposed to be completed within nine months. At the seven-month mark of the implementation, it was determined that the effort would need to be extended. The Executive Steering Committee remained strangely silent during the decision-making process, and very little effort was made by the program team to identify risks (i.e. incompatible architectural components, data migration issues, poor transition plans, etc.) and develop meaningful strategies to deal with those risks. With a major holiday approaching, the manufacturer is now expediting the implementation by adding more resources to the team with the intent of meeting the original nine-month timeframe and of not impacting the major sales season.

The addition of the extra resources was the solution necessary to meet the original timeframe. The implementation was completed following a 'big bang' approach just two months before the busiest holiday season of the year. Unfortunately, the implementation caused a widespread system outage and required a complete release back-out. The company's only choice at this point was to utilize the old systems. This created a massive backlog of manufacturing orders, unhappy angry customers and lost orders.

The Five Anchors

Anchor	Discussion
I. Strategic Alignment: IT Services to Business Objectives	
1. What are the business strategy, goals and objectives? *Are there any measures that*	• While every organization will have some strategy defined, we don't know what it is here. Know that any solution should link to

Anchor	Discussion
demonstrate the achievement of the business strategy, goals and objectives?	the achievement of the enterprise strategy, goals and objectives.
2. What is the business issue, or activity at risk?	• Production and shipment of the organization's product line during peak sales season.
3. Is the ownership to resolve the issue at the appropriate level of authority?	• Unknown, but the Executive Steering Committee for some unknown reason went silent during a crucial IT decision. Where is Change Management?
II. Security, Compliance, and Risk Issues	
1. Has there been a compromise of the information security policy?	• Unknown with the information provided.
2. What are the internal and external compliance or regulatory concerns?	• Certainly there are regulatory or compliance issues that need to be addressed. The main issue though is the contractual obligations with the customer.
3. What is the cultural appetite for risk?	• We assume there is discussion around the underpinning environment but the Executive Steering Committee (and any Change Management system) certainly ignored any known corporate culture for risk. • **COBIT5**: APO12, BAI06 • **ISO20K**: 4.1, 4.5.2, 4.5.3, 5.2, 6.3 • **ITIL**: SD 4.4, 4.6, 4.7, M, N.3; ST 4.2, 4.6

Anchor	Discussion
III. Value-based Portfolio	
1. Does the current portfolio meet expectations and needs of the stakeholder?	• Unknown with the information provided.
2. What is the value of that business activity (VBF)?	• This is their core business. Without this system, product is not being shipped therefore the potential and probability for sales and customer loss is high.
3. Does the portfolio have the right mix of resources to deliver business benefit?	• Assuming yes; the target delivery date was met, there were no other indications of failure or poor performance (other than the future massive failure).
IV. Design and Architecture	
1. Will the current architecture effectively resolve the issue? Is it feasible?	• Unknown with the information provided.
2. Can the current architecture accommodate the issue?	• Unknown with the information provided.
3. Do we have the necessary competencies to design the required change(s)?	• The assumption is yes. The current staff were able to meet the deadline and deal with all the moving parts of deploying a new ERP system. What was lacking was a thoughtful assessment of what could go wrong and have mitigating plans prepared.

Anchor	Discussion
V. Planning and Use of Resources	
1. What resources are required to resolve the situation (e.g. people, capital, technical...)?	• Better project planning where exceptions are considered and a more realistic view of time and resource necessary for the roll-out. This could have been accomplished by a better charter within the Executive Steering Group where proper oversight is forefront as well as their demand of the project team to report progress appropriately. • **COBIT5**: EDM03, APO12, BAI01, BAI03, BAI06, BAI07 • **ISO20K**: 5.0 • **ITIL**: ST 4.2, 4.4, 4.5, 4.6
2. Can the required resources be acquired?	• The assumption would be yes.
3. Is the necessary data and information available, collected and managed to resolve the current situation and prevent future occurrence?	• Unknown with the information provided.

Improvement Model Application

This scenario really falls into an "esoteric" category – it points directly at understanding the organizational tolerance toward risk, having the management leadership to control how projects are performed and having a robust Change Management process. It's really a cultural issue where process has not been designed (followed?) to ensure minimal impact of change. There are many process areas where one could focus; the main culprits are the overall management system, governance and Change Management.

The main improvement model would be COBIT5's Implementation Model – Phase 1 of this model "What are the drivers?" includes a failed IT initiative among others (e.g. internal or external events, trends, poor performance, etc.).The main outcome of Phase 1 is the development of a business case written for the executive management level and this case will be managed and monitored to ensure a successful outcome. This would have been of great use to the Executive Steering Committee in guiding their actions and decisions.

The tangible application of the Implementation Model comes in Phase 2, "Where are we now?", which links IT objectives with enterprise strategies and risks. This linkage defines the critical processes necessary for successful outcomes. Now we have a defined objective, clearly linking the necessary IT capabilities with the achievement of business outcome. This very action should have provided the necessary governance and oversight so that some of the "cowboy" activities would have been curtailed.

The underpinning policy in any service management framework is the control by the change management process. ISO/IEC 20000-1 unequivocally states the process of design and transition of new or changed services shall be managed via the change management policy and process. Period. The ultimate in control, at least as long as the process is robust enough and followed. If it's not, well, that's another issue that must be addressed and quickly (and in a different book!).

Solution References:

Primary Solution

Both COBIT5 and ISO/IEC 20000-1 drive the service manager to understand the risk appetite and then define and mitigate risk within those parameters. The SMS and the principles defined in the design and transition process demand it and manage those via change management. COBIT5 has defined specific processes around risk and change to ensure the intended outcome is achieved.

Secondary Solution

ITIL: All ST processes, especially "true" Change Management, control risk. Change Evaluation evaluates the benefits of a new or changed service from the "as planned/to be delivered" perspective and reports not only on the achievement of service requirements but also risk (specifically, residual risk). Their recommendations are submitted to Change Management for consideration in the "go/no-go" decision at key points in the transition cycle.

CHAPTER 7:
CASELET #4 – ACHIEVE BUSINESS OUTCOMES

IT Issue: A small auto insurance company has experienced significant growth in the last several years. The IT department has done a good job of managing increasing capacity requirements based on the demand patterns. Additionally, they provide an onsite service desk as well as level 2 and level 3 support and a fairly active PMO. In a strategic planning session held last year, the company leadership made it very clear that there were three vital areas which the IT department needed to focus on: 1) communication technologies must have high availability, 2) downtime of critical services must be kept to a minimum, and 3) customers need a self-help portal that provides value.

The IT department deployed all of the necessary technologies to support the stated vital needs of the business (as well as continued support of the core business functions), but continually had issues around supporting those services. The following issues have been identified in the last six months:

- The self-help portal doesn't provide information for the most commonly used services.
   o It is rarely used due to a poor design.
- Incident and request ticket backlog has grown by 120%.
- Three major incidents have occurred resulting in large amounts of downtime to critical services; one failure caused a 12-hour outage within their mobile communication technologies.

The Five Anchors

Anchor	Discussion
I. Strategic Alignment: IT Services to Business Objectives	
1. What are the business strategy, goals and objectives? *Are there any measures that demonstrate the achievement of the business strategy, goals and objectives?*	• The continued growth of the business is paramount but no specific business goals or objectives have been stated. What has been communicated is that IT must provide high availability, reduce the downtime of the critical services (implying the creation or improvement of a continuity plan) and provide a method of self-help. No measures are mentioned but could be easily created as necessary.
2. What is the business issue, or activity at risk?	• There are two issues – first the downtime of the critical services, which needs to be addressed not only from an agreed delivery position (i.e. SLAs and appropriate availability requirements and planning) but also from the intangible cost perspectives (i.e. confidence, reputation, etc.) all of which can lead to a loss of customers. Big question: Is there an IT Service Continuity plan? The second issue is one of poor support (backlog of incident and request tickets as well as major incidents). • **COBIT5**: BAI04 • **ISO20K**: 5.0, 6.3, 6.5 • **ITIL**: SD 4.4, 4.5, 4.6

Anchor	Discussion
3. Is the ownership to resolve the issue at the appropriate level of authority?	• Unclear, though organizational leadership did communicate what IT was to accomplish – we do not know the roles within IT but could assume a "like" position or direct report to the company leadership received those requests and then assigned as appropriate.
II. Security, Compliance, and Risk Issues	
1. Has there been a compromise of the information security policy?	• Unknown with the information provided.
2. What are the internal and external compliance or regulatory concerns?	• There are regulatory concerns within auto insurance companies, but the caselet does not hint that there have been any issues. But, this is a constraint for any planning of new or changed services to ensure continued compliance to the internal or external regulatory concerns or contractual obligations. • **COBIT5**: APO11, MEA03
3. What is the cultural appetite for risk?	• The organization has experienced growth and we've assumed they do want to continue that pattern. Logically, one can make a case that the strong growth pattern is a result of taking some risks to gain market share, thus the organization may be willing to accept some level of risk.

Anchor	Discussion
III. Value-based Portfolio	
1. Does the current portfolio meet expectations and needs of the stakeholder?	• The portfolio meets the needs of the organization if only due to the successful growth. The issues now seem to revolve around operational demand and support and the lack of a continuity plan (remember the 12-hour outage). IT should be analyzing the trends of use, develop/improve a continuity plan, and ensure appropriate knowledge and resources for the design and support staff.
2. What is the value of that business activity (VBF)?	• For the auto insurance industry, communication is vital for new policies, claims and policy management. The outages within communication technology directly affect the viability of this company. This IT organization would benefit from completing a Business Impact Analysis (BIA), if it hasn't been done already, to quantify and qualify the impact of the IT service loss. • **ITIL**: SD 4.6.5.2 (BIA)
3. Does the portfolio have the right mix of resources to deliver business benefit?	• Logically, we have to assume yes, if only because of the growth that has been managed to date (i.e. necessary functionality has been delivered). The current issues are more support process-oriented, rather than a non-functional service, specifically around the backlog of incidents and requests as well as the under-used and poorly designed self-help portal.

Anchor	Discussion
IV. Design and Architecture	
1. Will the current architecture effectively resolve the issue? Is it feasible?	• In the balancing of resources and capabilities, we assume they have the resources but capabilities may be lacking (i.e. management, processes, knowledge, organization and people). The current self-help portal is obviously not effective, thus requiring a major change. It is assumed the IT organization will require additional resources and capabilities for that project.
2. Can the current architecture accommodate the issue?	• There is no evidence the current architecture cannot overcome the issues.
3. Do we have the necessary competencies to design the required change(s)?	• Unknown at this point – but there are two pertinent facts: 1) IT has been able to keep up with the capacity demands; 2) IT has done a very poor job in designing a self-help system. Thus, IT leadership should define and re-examine current competencies, especially around the support area, and improve where necessary. • **COBIT5**: APO07 • **ISO20K**: 4.4 • **ITIL**: SS 6.10, SD 6.5, ST 6.6, SO 6.9, CSI 6.6 • **SFIA** *www.sfia.org.uk*
V. Planning and Use of Resources	
1. What resources are required to resolve	• Clearly, this IT organization needs to take a strong look at their support processes as well as

Anchor	Discussion
the situation (e.g. people, capital, technical...)?	the flexibility and continuity of their designs to address continued demand and mitigate the outages. Resource management practices need a review – has the company growth exceeded IT capacity? Additionally, a knowledge base for the self-help portal requires development and on-going maintenance for applicability. • **COBIT5**: BAI04, BAI08, DSS02, DSS04 • **ISO20K**: 4.4., 4.5, 5.0, 6.3, 8.1 • **ITIL**: SD 4.4, 4.6; ST 4.7; SO 4.2
2. Can the required resources be acquired?	• Without a doubt. The organizational sourcing model is unknown but current technologies are available to resolve the issues as long as this organization clearly defines the requirements before engaging a commercial solution (e.g. outsource the service desk, commercial tools to create the self-help portal, etc.). • **COBIT5**: APO10 • **ISO20K**: 7.2 • **ITIL**: SS 3.7, SD 3.11, 4.8
3. Is the necessary data and information available, collected and managed to resolve the current situation and prevent future occurrence?	• Clearly, there is some data available as we know of the poor use of the self-help portal, backlogs and outages. Is it being used to create a solution and or prevent future occurrence? That is unknown. • **COBIT5**: Information Enabler • **ISO20K**: 6.2 • **ITIL**: CSI 4.1

Improvement Model Application

This entire scenario screams "Process improvement!" and ITIL's CSI Approach and Seven-Step Improvement process would be an excellent fit to effectively and efficiently guide the necessary improvements. It is obvious the current practices are not keeping up with current business requirements and damaging overall business operations. To apply the CSI Model, confirmation of organizational goals and objectives is necessary ("What is the vision?") as well as a clearly defined future state ("Where do we want to be?") *before* the development of process and service improvements ("How do we get there?"). Remember, this organization already has some measures for its current state (we will not make a value judgment if those measures are sufficient).

These steps clearly relate to the Seven-Step Improvement Process, which really focuses on the collection of appropriate data to support improvement efforts. This process demands a very clear structure around the whole activity of data collection and analysis creating repeatable measures which drives reliability. Deploying this process would serve the organization well - if they are to continue to grow, developing consistency around the information upon which decisions are made, will serve them well.

Solution References:

Primary Solution:

ISO20K and ITIL: Review the requirements for Incident and Service Request Management (8.1) defined in ISO/IEC 20000-1 and consider the other practices described in ITIL around incidents and service requests. Also review the clear and concise process in ISO/IEC 20000-1 for the design and transition of new or changed services (it can be applied to process improvement as well) and go back and "fill in" the missing parts to create a better self-help portal as well as critically review the availability designs. ITIL offers expanded information in several areas:

- SD 3.0. 4.4; SO 4.2, 4.3; CSI 4.1

As recommended above, strongly consider the review and update of IT staff competencies and invest in their continued growth. SFIA offers a globally accepted framework for defining the various roles and competencies.

Secondary Solution:

Utilize the information within COBIT5 (as listed above) to guide metric development as well as appropriate relationships and communication between processes and stakeholders utilizing the RACI diagrams.

CHAPTER 8:
CASELET #5 – COMPLIANCE AND IMPROVEMENT

IT Issue: Last year, in an effort to get better visibility of assets in the company, a publicly traded energy company created a small IT team to manage the PC asset register. The intent of the team was to document the acquisition of PCs and assign ownership to each. Additionally, the software installed on each PC was managed via a software licensing contract ensuring up-to-date versions. This contract also documented the number of licenses distributed throughout the energy company for billing purposes.

In a recent internal asset audit, the team discovered that out of the 3000 PCs in the register, 300 had not been on the network in the last nine months (most of these were laptops), and it was unknown who had them or their locations. Upon learning this, the IT Director quickly held a meeting in which the following concerns were raised:

- It is unknown whether the 300 PCs have been lost, stolen, or simply being used in the field without having connected to the company's network.
- Sensitive information could be on the PCs.
- Since these have not been on the network in the last nine months, their anti-virus software could be out of date.
- The company is paying for licenses on PCs that are not being used.

The Five Anchors

Anchor	Discussion
I. Strategic Alignment: IT Services to Business Objectives	
1. What are the business strategy, goals and objectives? *Are there any measures that*	• Unknown with the information provided.

Anchor	Discussion
demonstrate the achievement of the business strategy, goals and objectives?	
2. What is the business issue, or activity at risk?	• Truly this an asset management issue. This organization has "lost" 10% of the purchased (or leased?) PCs and the impact is far beyond the actual physical device. There should be concerns around corporate data (data confidentiality), actual loss of corporate property and payment of license and potential maintenance fees.
3. Is the ownership to resolve the issue at the appropriate level of authority?	• The IT Director is now aware of the issue and it would be presumed there would be an appropriate delegation of this issue with the IT Director continuing in the accountable role.
II. Security, Compliance, and Risk Issues	
1. Has there been a compromise of the information security policy?	• While the caselet doesn't directly state this is an issue, the possibility is very real. • **COBIT5**: APO13, BAI09, DSS05 • **ISO20K**: 6.6, 9.1 • **ITIL**: SD 4.7; ST 4.3
2. What are the internal and external compliance or regulatory concerns?	• As a publically traded company, there are numerous regulatory, statutory and legal concerns (as well as potential contractual obligations). A primary concern within a majority of the

Anchor	Discussion
	regulations includes positive control of company information assets (i.e. safeguarding of customer information, etc.). • **COBIT5**: APO11, MEA03 • **ISO20K**: 4.1 • **ITIL**: 4.1
3. What is the cultural appetite for risk?	• The nature of the organization would presume a low risk appetite in some areas and others (trading) may have a much higher appetite. What is important to know from an IT perspective and for this specific issue, is understanding what potential information and services are at risk and the overall vulnerability to the energy company.
III. Value-based Portfolio	
1. Does the current portfolio meet expectations and needs of the stakeholder?	• Unknown with the information provided.
2. What is the value of that business activity (VBF)?	• Unknown with the information provided.
3. Does the portfolio have the right mix of resources to deliver business benefit?	• Unknown with the information provided.

Anchor	Discussion
IV. Design and Architecture	
1. Will the current architecture effectively resolve the issue? Is it feasible?	• The process architecture demands improvement. There seems to be some level of control of the infrastructure and there is no indication of outage or compromise. But, the issue clearly is one of asset management and the lack of process that will maintain control over corporate assets. • Therefore, the IT Director (or delegate to an appropriate party) should deploy good Problem Management techniques and discover why these 300 laptops have gone missing. Use this information to improve the asset management processes. • **COBIT5**: BAI09, DSS03 • **ISO20K**: 4.5.4, 4.5.5, 8.2, 9.1 • **ITIL**: CSI 4.1
2. Can the current architecture accommodate the issue?	• Presumably. It seems there is some level of control and management – the current issue doesn't seem to be chronic.
3. Do we have the necessary competencies to design the required change(s)?	• The small IT team was able to create a PC asset register and collect current information. What is lacking now are the overall controls necessary to ensure equipment is properly identified, controlled, deployed and managed. • **COBIT5**: BAI06, BAI07, BAI09, BAI10 • **ISO20K**: 9.1, 9.2, 9.3 • **ITIL**: ST 4.2, 4.3, 4.4

Anchor	Discussion
V. Planning and Use of Resources	
1. What resources are required to resolve the situation (e.g. people, capital, technical...)?	• The IT Director must recognize the process improvements will require funding as well as appropriate training or even re-training.
2. Can the required resources be acquired?	• It shouldn't be an issue as long as the leadership recognizes the impact of the missing PCs to the overall market standing of the organization. This event is not something that should be "swept under the rug" and ignored, even though the full impact is not stated in the caselet.
3. Is the necessary data and information available, collected and managed to resolve the current situation and prevent future occurrence?	• The organization has collected the data and is beginning the investigation into a resolution. We would assume once the IT Director's concerns were answered there would be specific changes to ensure the cause is remedied and monitored.

Improvement Model Application

The scenario circumstances describe an organization that recognizes there is a need to improve their asset management practices. We don't know if there has been any business impact. We have seen steps in the IT department that truly follow the elements of PDCA and they should continue that journey. What they should add is a clearly defined policy around the management of the PCs – we have seen over and over again in industry, PCs going missing because of lax controls when it comes time to upgrade. These actions can be easily translated across the enterprise as necessary.

Solution References:

Primary Solution:

All three frameworks offer support in the solution – ISO/IEC 20000-1 provides the detail around the application of a PDCA management system, ITIL provides detail around the necessary elements of asset management and components of a security policy and COBIT specifies required governance factors. As a solution is developed, this organization needs to ensure the regulatory, statutory or other legal requirements are met. Lastly, even if IT "gets their asset house in order," it will make absolutely no difference if the new policies are not endorsed by top management and communicated to the user community – this is not just an IT issue! IT should take the lead, but it is an enterprise compliance issue and it should be treated as such.

APPENDIX: THE MAP

Using the domains and processes within COBIT5, we have created a mapping between ISO/IEC 20000-1:2011 and ITIL 2011. Before jumping in and exploring the mapping, a few disclaimers are necessary:

- Processes in COBIT5 are not discrete when compared to ISO/IEC 20000-1 and ITIL – you may very well "see" alternate relationships.
- The numbers in the ITIL and ISO/IEC 20000-1:2011 columns are based on section numbering within the source documents. Those numbers are reproduced in Tables 1, 2 and 3 in Chapter 2.
- Relationships are based on process and sub-process activity descriptions in COBIT5, where it is not uncommon to see activities from multiple ITIL and 20K processes.
- Processes that have been noted in parenthesis are minor relationships.
- Where only the ITIL volume name is provided, the specific COBIT5 activity is assumed or underpins the entire ITIL phase.
- Supporting frameworks, standards or methodologies are listed in bold and red.

Appendix: The Map

Legend for acronyms:

Acronym	Process Name (ITIL volume)
7S	7-step Improvement Process (CSI)
AcM	Access Management (SO)
AM	Availability Management (SD)
AppM	*Application Management (SO)**
BRM	Business Relationship Management (SS)
CapM	Capacity Management (SD)
ChE	Change Evaluation (ST)
ChM	Change Management (ST)
CSI	**Continual Service Improvement****
DC	Design Coordination (SD)
DM	Demand Management (SS)
EM	Event Management (SO)
FM	Financial Management for IT Services (SS)
IM	Incident Management (SO)
ISM	Information Security Management (SD)
ITOM	*IT Operations Management (SO)**
ITSCM	IT Service Continuity Management (SD)
KM	Knowledge Management (ST)
PM	Problem Management (SO)
RDM	Release and Deployment Management (ST)
RF	Request Fulfillment (SO)
SACM	Service Asset and Configuration Management (ST)
ScatM	Service Catalogue Management (SD)
SD	**Service Design****
	*Service Desk (SO)**
SLM	Service Level Management (SD)
SO	**Service Operation****
SPM	Service Portfolio Management (SS)
SS	**Service Strategy****
ST	**Service Transition****
StM	Strategy Management for IT Services (SS)
SuppM	Supplier Management (SD)
SVT	Service Validation and Testing (ST)
TM	*Technical Management (SO)**
TPS	Transition Planning and Support (ST)

Notes: Service Desk will not be abbreviated owing to possible confusion with the Service Design volume.

*Functions **The ITIL volume

70

Evaluate, Direct & Monitor (EDM)		ITIL	ISO/IEC20000-1:2011
01	**Ensure Governance Framework Setting & Maintenance (ISO/IEC 38500)**		
.01	Evaluate the Governance System	SS 5.1 (4.1, 4.2); CSI 3.10	4.1
.02	Direct the Governance System	SS 5.1 (4.1)	4.1
.03	Monitor the Governance System	SS 5.1 (4.1)	4.1, 4.5
02	**Ensure Benefits Delivery**		
.01	Evaluate Value Optimization	SS 3.2.3, 4.1, 4.2, 4.5	4.1, 4.2, 7.1, 7.2
.02	Direct Value Optimization	SS 3.2.3, 4.2, 4.5	4.1, 7.1
.03	Monitor Value Optimization	SS 4.1, 4.2; SD 4.3, CSI	4.1, 4.5.4, 6.2
03	**Ensure Risk Optimization (ISO/IEC 31000)**		
.01	Evaluate risk management	SS 4.2, 5.6.5, D.3, E	4.1.1
.02	Direct risk management	SS 4.2; SD 4.3, 4.6, 4.7	4.5.5.2
.03	Monitor risk management	SS 4.2	4.5.3
04	**Ensure Resource Optimization (SFIA)**		
.01	Evaluate resource management	SS 5.1, 5.2, 6.10 (4.1, 4.2)	4.1, 4.4
.02	Direct resource management	SS 6.10 (4.2)	4.1, 4.4
.03	Monitor resource management	SS 6.10 (4.2)	4.1, 4.4
05	**Ensure Stakeholder Transparency**		
.01	Evaluate Stakeholder reporting requirements	CSI 5.7 (SS 4.5; SD 6.3)	4.1, 6.2
.02	Direct stakeholder communication & reporting	ST 5.1 (SS 4.5; SD 6.3)	4.1, 6.1, 6.2, 7.1
.03	Monitor stakeholder communication	SS 4.5; SD 6.3 (ST 5.1)	4.1, 6.1, 6.2, 7.1

		ITIL	ISO/IEC20000-1:2011
Align, Plan & Organize (APO)			
01	**Manage the IT Management Framework**		
.01	Define the organizational structure	(SS 4.1)	4.1
.02	Establish roles and responsibilities	(SS 4.1)	4.1, 4.4
.03	Maintain the enablers of the management system	(SS 4.1)	4.1
.04	Communicate management objectives and direction	(SS 4.1)	4.1
.05	Optimize the placement of the IT function	(SS 4.1)	4.1
.06	Define information (data) and system ownership	(SS 4.1)	4.1, 4.3
.07	Manage continual improvement of processes	(SS 4.1)	4.1, 4.5
.08	Maintain compliance with policies and procedures	All	4.1
02	**Manage Strategy**		
.01	Understand enterprise direction	SS 4.1 (4.2, 4.5)	(4.1, 4.5)
.02	Assess the current environment, capabilities and performance	SS 4.1 (4.2, 4.5)	(4.1, 4.5)
.03	Define the target IT capabilities	SS 4.1 (4.2, 4.5)	(4.1, 4.5)
.04	Conduct a gap analysis	SS 4.1 (4.2, 4.5)	(4.1, 4.5)
.05	Define the strategic plan and road map	SS 4.1 (4.2, 4.5)	(4.1, 4.5)
.06	Communicate the IT strategy and direction	SS 4.1 (4.2, 4.5)	4.1
03	**Manage Enterprise Architecture**		
.01	Develop the enterprise architecture vision	SO 6.4; (SS, SD)	(4.0, 5.0)
.02	Define reference architecture	SO 6.4; (SS, SD)	(4.0, 5.0)
.03	Select opportunities and solutions	SS 4.1, 4.2; CSI (SO 6.4)	(4.0, 5.0)
.04	Define architecture implementation	SO 6.4; (SS, SD)	(4.0, 5.0)
.05	Provide enterprise architecture services	SO 6.4; (SS, SD)	(4.0, 5.0)

Align, Plan & Organize (APO)		ITIL	ISO/IEC20000-1:2011
04	**Manage Innovation**		
.01	Create an environment conducive to innovation	(SS, SD, ST goal)	
.02	Maintain an understanding of the enterprise environment	SS 4.5; SD 6.3	
.03	Monitor and scan the technology environment	SD 4.5 (SS 4.2)	6.5
.04	Assess the potential of emerging technologies and innovation ideas	SD 4.5; ST 4.2	6.5
.05	Recommend appropriate further initiatives	SD 4.5; ST 4.2	6.5
.06	Monitor the implementation and use of innovation	(SS 4.2)	
05	**Manage Portfolio**		
.01	Establish the target investment mix	SS 4.2 (4.3, 4.4)	(4.0, 5.0, 6.4)
.02	Determined the availability and sources of funds	SS 4.2 (4.3)	(4.0, 5.0, 6.4)
.03	Evaluate and select programs to fund	SS 4.2 (4.3, 4.4)	(4.0, 5.0, 6.4)
.04	Monitor, optimize and report on investment portfolio performance	SS 4.2 (SS 4.3; CSI)	(4.0, 5.0, 6.4)
.05	Maintain portfolios	SS 4.2 (4.3)	(4.0, 5.0, 6.4)
.06	Manage benefits achievement	SS 4.2 (4.3)	(4.0, 5.0, 6.4)
06	**Manage Budget & Costs**		
.01	Manage finance and accounting	SS 4.3	6.4
.02	Prioritize resource allocation	SS 4.2, 4.3	6.4
.03	Create and maintain budgets	SS 4.3 (4.1)	6.4
.04	Model and allocate costs	SS 4.3	6.4
.05	Manage costs	SS 4.3	6.4
07	**Manage Human Resources**		
.01	Maintain adequate and appropriate staffing	SD 4.5; SO 6.3-6.6	4.4, 6.5
.02	Identify key IT personnel	ST 4.7 (SS 4.2)	4.4
.03	Maintain the skills and competencies of personnel	ST 4.7, 6.6	4.4
.04	Evaluate employee job performance	(ST 6.6)	4.4
.05	Plan and track the usage of IT and business human resources	SS 4.2	
.06	Manage contract staff	SD 4.8; SO 6.4-6.6	7.2

Align, Plan & Organize (APO)	ITIL	ISO/IEC20000-1:2011
08 Manage Relationships		
.01 Understand business expectations	SS 4.5 (4.4; SD 4.3)	7.1
.02 Identify opportunities, risk and constraints for IT to enhance the business	SS 4.5 (SD 4.5)	6.5, 7.1
.03 Manage the business relationship	SS 4.5; SD 4.3	6.1, 7.1
.04 Coordinate and communicate	SD 4.3 (SS 4.5)	6.1 (7.1)
.05 Provide input to the continual improvement of services	SS 4.5; SD 4.3; CSI	6.1, 7.1
09 Manage Service Agreements		
.01 Identify IT services	SD 4.2, 4.3 (SS 4.2, 4.4)	6.1
.02 Catalogue IT-enabled services	SD 4.2 (SS 4.2)	6.1
.03 Define and prepare service agreements	SD 4.3, 4.8 (SS 4.2)	6.1, 7.2
.04 Monitor and report service levels	SD 4.3 (SD 4.5; SO, CSI)	6.1, 6.2
.05 Review service agreements and contracts	SD 4.3, 4.8	6.1, 7.2
10 Manage Suppliers		
.01 Identify and evaluate supplier relationships and contracts	SD 4.8 (SS 4.2)	7.2
.02 Select suppliers	SD 4.8	7.2
.03 Manage supplier relationships & contracts	SD 4.8	4.2, 6.1, 7.2
.04 Manage supplier risk	SD 4.8	4.2, 7.2
.05 Monitor supplier performance and compliance	SD 4.8, 4.3	4.2, 7.2
11 Manage Quality (ISO 9001)		
.01 Establish a quality management system (QMS)	CSI A.2 (SS 4.5; CSI)	(4.0)
.02 Define and manage quality standards practices and procedures	Implied CSI	(4.0)
.03 Focus quality management on customers	Implied CSI	(4.0)
.04 Perform quality monitoring, control and reviews	Implied CSI	(4.0)
.05 Integrate a quality management into solutions for development and service delivery	Implied CSI	(4.0)
.06 Maintain continuous improvement	Implied CSI	4.5.5

		ITIL	ISO/IEC20000-1:2011
Align, Plan & Organize (APO)			
12	**Manage Risk (ISO/IEC 31000)**		
.01	Collect data	SD 4.4, 4.6, 4.7, M, N.3; ST 4.2, 4.6	4.1, 4.5, 5.0, 6.3, 6.6, 9.2
.02	Analyze risk	SD 4.4, 4.6, 4.7, M, N.3; ST 4.2, 4.6	4.1, 4.5, 5.0, 6.3, 6.6, 9.2
.03	Maintain a risk profile	Lifecycle activities	4.1, 4.5, 5.0, 6.3, 6.6, 9.2
.04	Articulate risk	ST 4.6	4.1, 4.5, 5.0, 6.3, 6.6, 9.2
.05	Define a risk management action portfolio	Lifecycle activities	4.1, 4.5, 5.0, 6.3, 6.6, 9.2
.06	Respond to risk	Lifecycle activities	4.1, 4.5, 5.0, 6.3, 6.6, 9.2
13	**Manage Security (ISO/IEC 27000)**		
.01	Establish and maintain an ISMS	SD 4.7	6.6
.02	Define and manage an information security risk treatment plan	SD 4.7	6.6
.03	Monitor and review the ISMS	SD 4.7	6.6

			ITIL	ISO/IEC20000-1:2011
01	**Build, Acquire & Implement (BAI)**			
		Manage Programs & Projects (PMI®; PRINCE2®; P3O®, Six Sigma)		
	.01	Maintain a standard approach for program and project management	(SS 4.2, 4.5, 6.7, D.10; CSI 4.1)	(4.5, 5.0)
	.02	Initiate a program	(SS 4.2, 4.5, 6.7, D.10; CSI 4.1)	(4.5, 5.0)
	.03	Manage stakeholder engagement	(SS 4.2, 4.5, 6.7, D.10; CSI 4.1)	(4.5, 5.0)
	.04	Develop and maintain the program	(SS 4.2, 4.5, 6.7, D.10; CSI 4.1)	(4.5, 5.0)
	.05	Launch and execute the program	(SS 4.2, 4.5, 6.7, D.10; CSI 4.1)	(4.5, 5.0)
	.06	Monitor, control and report on the program outcomes	(SS 4.2, 4.5, 6.7, D.10; CSI 4.1)	(4.5, 5.0)
	.07	Start up and initiate projects within a program	(SS 4.2, 4.5, 6.7, D.10; CSI 4.1)	(4.5, 5.0)
	.08	Plan projects	(SS 4.2, 4.5, 6.7, D.10; CSI 4.1)	(4.5, 5.0)
	.09	Manage program and project quality	(SS 4.2, 4.5, 6.7, D.10; CSI 4.1)	(4.5, 5.0)
	.10	Manage program and project risk	(SS 4.2, 4.5, 6.7, D.10; CSI 4.1)	(4.5, 5.0)
	.11	Monitor and control projects	(SS 4.2, 4.5, 6.7, D.10; CSI 4.1)	(4.5, 5.0)
	.12	Manage project resources and work packages	(SS 4.2, 4.5, 6.7, D.10; CSI 4.1)	(4.5, 5.0)
	.13	Close a project or iteration	(SS 4.2, 4.5, 6.7, D.10; CSI 4.1)	(4.5, 5.0)
	.14	Close a program	(SS 4.2, 4.5, 6.7, D.10; CSI 4.1)	(4.5, 5.0)
02	**Manage Requirements Definition**			
	.01	Define and maintain business functional and technical requirements	SD 3.4, 3.5, 4.3, 5.1; (SS 4.5)	5.2
	.02	Perform a feasibility study and formulate alternative solutions	SD 3.8.1	(5.2)
	.03	Manage requirements risks	(SD)	5.2
	.04	Obtain approval of requirements and solutions	SD 4.3	5.2

		ITIL	ISO/IEC20000-1:2011
03	**Build, Acquire & Implement (BAI)**		
	Manage Solutions Identification & Build		
.01	Design high-level solutions	SD 4.1, 4.4, 4.5, 4.6; SO 6.4, 6.5, 6.6	5.3
.02	Design detailed solution components	SD 4.1, 4.4, 4.5, 4.6; SO 6.4, 6.5, 6.6	5.3
.03	Develop solution components	SD 4.4; SO 6.4, 6.5, 6.6	5.3
.04	Procure solution components	SS 4.3, SD 4.4, 4.8; SO 6.4, 6.5, 6.6	5.3
.05	Build solutions	ST 4.1, 4.4; SO 6.4, 6.5, 6.6	5.3
.06	Perform quality assurance	ST 4.4, 4.5, 4.6; SO 6.4, 6.5, 6.6	5.3
.07	Prepare for solution testing	ST 4.5 (4.4); SO 6.4, 6.5, 6.6	5.3
.08	Execute solution testing	ST 4.5 (4.4); SO 6.4, 6.5, 6.6	5.3
.09	Manage changes to requirements	ST 4.2 (SD 6.3; SS 4.5); SO 6.4, 6.5, 6.6	5.3
.10	Maintain solutions	ST 4.2, 4.3, 4.4; SO 6.4, 6.5, 6.6	5.3
.11	Define IT services and maintain the service portfolio	SS 4.2; SD 4.2, 4.3; ST 4.2; SO 6.4, 6.5, 6.6	5.3
04	**Manage Availability & Capacity**		
.01	Assess current availability, performance and capacity and create a baseline	SD 4.4, 4.5	6.3, 6.4
.02	Assess business impact	SD 4.4, 4.5 (4.3, 4.6); ST 4.2	6.3, 6.4; 9.2
.03	Plan for new or changed service requirements	SD 4.4, 4.5; ST 4.2; CSI	6.3, 6.4
.04	Monitor and review availability and capacity	SD 4.4, 4.5	6.3, 6.4
.05	Investigate and address availability, performance and capacity issues	SD 4.4, 4.5; SO 4.4	6.3, 6.4, 8.2
05	**Manage Organizational Change Enablement**		
.01	Establish the desire to change	ST 4.2, 5.2, C.11 (4.4)	4.1, 5.3
.02	Form an effective implementation team	ST 4.2, 5.2, C.11 (4.4)	
.03	Communicate desired vision	ST 4.2, 5.2, C.11 (4.4)	4.1
.04	Empower role players and identify short-term wins	ST 4.2, 5.2, C.11 (4.4)	
.05	Enable operation and use	ST 4.2, 5.2, C.11 (4.4)	5.3
.06	Embed new approaches	ST 4.2, 4.7. 5.2, C.11 (4.4)	
.07	Sustain changes	ST 4.2, 4.7, 5.2, C.11 (4.4)	

Build, Acquire & Implement (BAI)		ITIL	ISO/IEC20000-1:2011
06	**Manage Changes**		
.01	Evaluate, prioritize and authorize change requests	ST 4.2	9.2
.02	Manage emergency changes	ST 4.2	9.2
.03	Track and report change status	ST 4.2	9.2
.04	Close and document the changes	ST 4.2	9.2
07	**Manage Change Acceptance & Transitioning**		
.01	Establish an implementation plan	ST 3.1, 4.4, 4.5; SO 4.4, 4.5, 4.6	9.3
.02	Plan business process, system and data conversion	ST 4.4; SO 4.4, 4.5, 4.6	9.3
.03	Plan acceptance test	SD 3.7; ST 4.4; SO 4.4, 4.5, 4.6	5.4, 9.3
.04	Establish a test environment	ST 4.4, 4.5; SO 4.4, 4.5, 4.6	5.4, 9.3
.05	Perform acceptance tests	ST 4.4, 4.5; SO 4.4, 4.5, 4.6	5.4, 9.3
.06	Promote to production and manage releases	ST 4.4; SO 4.4, 4.5, 4.6	9.3
.07	Provide early production support	ST 4.4; SO 4.4, 4.5, 4.6	9.3
.08	Perform a post-implementation review	ST 4.2, 4.4; SO 4.4, 4.5, 4.6	9.2
08	**Manage Knowledge**		
.01	Nurture and facilitate a knowledge-sharing culture	ST 4.7, 7.1	4.3
.02	Identify and classify sources of information	ST 4.7, 7.1	4.3
.03	Organize and contextualize information into knowledge	ST 4.7, 7.1	4.3
.04	Use and share knowledge	ST 4.7, 7.1 (4.4)	4.3
.05	Evaluate and retire information	ST 4.7, 7.1	4.3

Build, Acquire & Implement (BAI)		ITIL	ISO/IEC20000-1:2011
09	**Manage Assets**		
.01	Identify and record current assets	ST 4.3	6.4, 9.1
.02	Manage critical assets	ST 4.3 (4.2)	6.4, 9.1
.03	Manage the asset lifecycle	ST 4.3 (4.2); (SS 4.3)	(6.4), 9.1, (9.2)
.04	Optimize asset costs	ST 4.3 (4.2); (SS 4.3)	(6.4), 9.1, (9.2)
.05	Manage licenses	ST 4.3	6.4, 9.1
10	**Manage Configuration**		
.01	Establish and maintain a configuration model	ST 4.3	9.1
.02	Establish and maintain a configuration repository and baseline	ST 4.3	9.1
.03	Maintain and control configuration items	ST 4.3 (4.2)	9.1
.04	Produce status and configuration reports	ST 4.3	9.1
.05	Verify and review integrity of the configuration repository	ST 4.3	9.1

Deliver, Service & Support (DSS)		ITIL	ISO/IEC20000-1:2011
01	**Manage Operations**		
.01	Perform operational procedures	SO 6.4, 6.5	
.02	Manage outsourced IT services	SD 4.8	7.2
.03	Monitor IT infrastructure	SO 4.1, 6.4, 6.5; (SD 4.4, 4.5)	6.3
.04	Manage the environment	SO 6.4, 6.5	
.05	Manage facilities	SO 6.4, 6.5	
02	**Manage Service Requests & Incidents**		
.01	Define incident and service request classification schemes	SO 4.2, 4.3 (SD 4.3)	8.1
.02	Record, classify and priorities request and incident	SO 4.2, 4.3, 6.3; SD 4.7 (4.3)	6.3, 8.1
.03	Verify, approve and fulfill service requests	SO 4.3, 6.4, 6.6	8.1
.04	Investigate, diagnose and allocate incidents	SO 4.2, 6.4, 6.6, (4.4)	8.1 (8.2)
.05	Resolve and recover from Incidents	SO 4.2, 6.4, 6.6	8.1
.06	Close service request and incidents	SO 4.2, 4.3, 6.3	8.1
.07	Track status and produce reports	SO 4.2, 4.3, 6.3	8.1
03	**Manage Problems**		
.01	Identify and classify problems	SO 4.4	8.2
.02	Investigate and diagnose problems	SO 4.4, 6.4, 6.6	8.2
.03	Raise known errors	SO 4.4, 6.4, 6.6	8.2
.04	Resolve and close problems	SO 4.4, 6.4, 6.6; (ST 4.2)	8.2 (9.2)
.05	Perform proactive problem management	SD 4.4; SO 4.4	6.3, 8.2

Deliver, Service & Support (DSS)	ITIL	ISO/IEC20000-1:2011
04 Manage Continuity		
.01 Define the business continuity policy, objectives and scope	SD 4.6	6.3
.02 Maintain a continuity strategy	SD 4.6	6.3
.03 Develop and implement a business continuity response	SD 4.6 (4.7)	6.3 (6.6)
.04 Exercise, test and review the BCP	SD 4.6	6.3
.05 Review, maintain and improve the continuity plan	SD 4.6 (4.3; SS 4.5)	6.3 (6.1, 7.1)
.06 Conduct continuity plan training	SD 4.6	6.3
.07 Manage backup arrangements	SD 4.6 (SO 6.4, 6.5)	6.3
.08 Conduct post-resumption review	SD 4.6	6.3
05 Manage Security Services (ISO/IEC 27001)		
.01 Protect against malware	SD 4.7	6.6
.02 Manage network and connectivity security	SD 4.7; SO 6.4; (ST 4.3)	6.6 (9.1)
.03 Manage endpoint security	SD 4.7; SO 6.4	6.6
.04 Manage user identity and logical access	SO 4.5 (SD 4.4, 4.7)	6.3, 6.6
.05 Manage physical access to IT assets	SD 4.7; SO 6.5	6.6
.06 Manage sensitive documents and output devices	SD 4.7; SO 6.5	4.3, 6.6
.07 Monitor the infrastructure for security-related events	SO 4.2; SD 4.7	6.6 (8.1)
06 Manage Business Process Controls		
.01 Align control activities embedded in business processes with enterprise objectives	(SS)	
.02 Control the processing of information	SD 4.7 (4.4; SO 4.5)	6.6
.03 Manage roles, responsibilities, access privileges and levels of authority	SD 4.4, 4.7; SO 4.5	6.6
.04 Manage errors and exceptions	SD 4.4, 4.7; SO 4.5	6.6
.05 Ensure traceability of information events and accountabilities	SD 4.4, 4.7; SO 4.5	6.6
.06 Secure information assets	SD 4.7; ST 4.7	4.3, 6.6

Monitor, Evaluate & Assess (MEA)

		ITIL	ISO/IEC20000-1:2011
01	**Monitor, Evaluate & Assess Performance & Conformance**		
.01	Establish a monitoring approach	SO 6.4, 6.5; CSI (SD 4.5)	4.5, 6.2
.02	Set performance and conformance targets	SO 6.4, 6.5; (SD 4.3, 4.5)	6.2
.03	Collect and process performance and conformance data	CSI 4.1, 5.4, 5.5, 5.7	6.2
.04	Analyze and report performance	CSI 4.1, 5.4, 5.5, 5.7	6.2
.05	Ensure the implementation of corrective actions	ST 4.2; CSI 4.1	5.0, 9.2
02	**Monitor, Evaluate & Assess the System of Internal Control**		
.01	Monitor internal controls	(SS, CSI)	4.5.4
.02	Review business process controls effectiveness	(SS, CSI)	4.5.4
.03	Perform control self-assessments	(SS, CSI)	4.5.4, 4.5.5, 6.2
.04	Identify and report control deficiencies	(SS, CSI)	4.5.4
.05	Ensure that assurance providers are independent and qualified	(SS, CSI)	4.5.4
.06	Plan assurance initiatives	(SS, CSI)	4.5.4
.07	Scope assurance initiatives	(SS, CSI)	4.5.4, 6.2
.08	Execute assurance initiatives	(SS, CSI)	4.5.4, 6.2
03	**Monitor, Evaluate & Assess Compliance with External Requirements**		
.01	Identify external compliance requirements	(SS, CSI)	4.1, 4.5, 6.5, 6.6
.02	Optimize response to external requirements	(SS, CSI)	4.1
.03	Confirm external compliance	(SS, CSI)	4.1
.04	Obtain assurance of external compliance	(SS, CSI)	4.5.4

ITG RESOURCES

IT Governance Ltd sources, creates and delivers products and services to meet the real-world, evolving IT governance needs of today's organisations, directors, managers and practitioners. The ITG website (*www.itgovernance.co.uk*) is the international one-stop-shop for corporate and IT governance information, advice, guidance, books, tools, training and consultancy.

www.itgovernance.co.uk/cobit.aspx is the information page on our website for COBIT resources. For ISO20000 resources please visit *www.itgovernance.co.uk/iso20000.aspx*, and for ITIL resources please visit *www.itgovernance.co.uk/itil.aspx*.

Other Websites

Books and tools published by IT Governance Publishing (ITGP) are available from all business booksellers and are also immediately available from the following websites:

www.itgovernance.eu is our euro-denominated website which ships from Benelux and has a growing range of books in European languages other than English.

www.itgovernanceusa.com is a US$-based website that delivers the full range of IT Governance products to North America, and ships from within the continental US.

www.itgovernance.in provides a selected range of ITGP products specifically for customers in the Indian sub-continent.

www.itgovernance.asia delivers the full range of ITGP publications, serving countries across Asia Pacific. Shipping from Hong Kong, US dollars, Singapore dollars, Hong Kong dollars, New Zealand dollars and Thai baht are all accepted through the website.

Toolkits

ITG's unique range of toolkits includes the IT Governance Framework Toolkit, which contains all the tools and guidance that you will need in order to develop and implement an appropriate IT governance framework for your organisation.

For a free paper on how to use the proprietary Calder-Moir IT Governance Framework, and for a free trial version of the toolkit, see *www.itgovernance.co.uk/calder_moir.aspx*.

There is also a wide range of toolkits to simplify implementation of management systems, such as an ISO/IEC 27001 ISMS or an ISO/IEC 22301 BCMS, and these can all be viewed and purchased online at *www.itgovernance.co.uk*.

Training Services

IT Governance offers an extensive portfolio of training courses designed to educate information security, IT governance, risk management and compliance professionals. Our classroom and online training programmes will help you develop the skills required to deliver best practice and compliance to your organisation. They will also enhance your career by providing you with industry standard certifications and increased peer recognition. Our range of courses offer a structured learning path from foundation to advanced level in the key topics of information security, IT governance, business continuity and service management.

ISO/IEC 20000 is the first International Standard for IT service management and has been developed to reflect the best practice guidance contained within the ITIL framework. Our ISO20000 Foundation and Practitioner training courses are designed to provide delegates with a comprehensive introduction and guide to the implementation of an ISO20000 management system and an industry recognised qualification awarded by APMG International. We also have a unique ITIL Foundation (2 Day) training course designed to provide delegates with the knowledge and skills required to pass the EXIN ITIL Foundation examination at the very first attempt. This classroom course has been specifically designed to ensure delegates acquire the ITIL Foundation Certificate at the lowest cost and with the least amount of time away from the office.

Full details of all IT Governance training courses can be found at *www.itgovernance.co.uk/training.aspx*.

Professional Services and Consultancy

Our expert consultants can show you how to best apply the lessons of ITIL, COBIT and ISO/IEC 20000 so that you can make process improvements and eliminate any 'gaps'. We explain the ideal and purpose behind each framework and then help you to find the most appropriate solutions to create a stronger and more robust Service Management System (SMS). By drawing on our extensive experience of management systems to combine service management frameworks, you can support the goal of delivering quality services that benefit the business - efficiently, effectively and economically.

We can coach you in the most effective ways to conduct enterprise-wide assessments. With our support, you will learn to describe the often complex interrelationships between different processes, recognizing and taking account of the various maturity levels.

Our consultants can also transfer the knowledge needed to successfully implement IT service management frameworks in line with international standards such as ISO9001, ISO/IEC 27001, ISO22301, ISO14001, and OHSAS18001. Through the integration of management systems in this way, you will be able to develop a comprehensive improvement approach that achieves high levels of quality across the whole enterprise.

For more information about IT Governance Consultancy for IT service management, see *www.itgovernance.co.uk/itsm-itil-iso20000-consultancy.aspx.*

Publishing Services

IT Governance Publishing (ITGP) is the world's leading IT-GRC publishing imprint that is wholly owned by IT Governance Ltd.

With books and tools covering all IT governance, risk and compliance frameworks, we are the publisher of choice for authors and distributors alike, producing unique and practical publications of the highest quality, in the latest formats available, which readers will find invaluable.

www.itgovernancepublishing.co.uk is the website dedicated to ITGP enabling both current and future authors, distributors, readers and other interested parties, to have easier access to more information. This allows ITGP website visitors to keep up to date with the latest publications and news.

Newsletter

IT governance is one of the hottest topics in business today, not least because it is also the fastest moving.

You can stay up to date with the latest developments across the whole spectrum of IT governance subject matter, including; risk management, information security, ITIL and IT service management, project governance, compliance and so much more, by subscribing to ITG's core publications and topic alert emails.

Simply visit our subscription centre and select your preferences: *www.itgovernance.co.uk/newsletter.aspx*.

9 781849 285148